THIS IS WYOMING
- LIVE -

A living interpretation of Wyoming -
A being with five faces

THE LAND - Surviving The Simple Life

THE PEOPLE - A Tough-tender Spirit

NATURE - Enchantment in The Ordinary

WILDLIFE - Getting to Know You

HISTORY - Peering into The Past

by Betty Starks Case

Cover photo by N.L. Case

(Cow moose at Brooks Lake)

LCCN: 00-140021
ISBN: 0-9706523-0-5

Printed and bound in the United States of America
by Pioneer Printing, Cheyenne, Wyoming 82003

Published by Windsong Books
P.O. Box 1355
Riverton, WY 82501
Phone: 1-307-856-5135

Also by Betty Starks Case

Maggie: Set Free in The Wyoming Rockies

For Ned

whose natural bonding with the land
led me to see the faces
of the wild and beautiful body of Wyoming

This is Wyoming
- Live -

Body, Spirit and History

by

Betty Starks Case

Betty Starks Case

Windsong Books

Table of Contents

Part III: Nature - Enchantment in The Ordinary

Part IV: Wildlife - Getting to Know You

ACKNOWLEDGMENTS

This book gives voice to the colorful, lively and sometimes dangerous spirit of Wyoming in stories born of an intimate association with the land, the people, nature, wildlife, and outstanding parts of state history. The stories reflect Wyoming life through my eyes and experiences, but could well be that of any Wyomingite or visitor who lives, loves and is fed by the mystery of this still wild and largely undefined land.

As with most non-fiction works, inspiration came from many directions. Bob and Steven Peck, publishers of The Ranger, an award-winning daily Wyoming newspaper, encouraged me for 14 years to continue telling stories of life in Wyoming. I thank them.

My gratitude goes to Cody Beers, Associate Editor of *Wyoming Wildlife*, who lent his philosophy to mine when he wrote in that popular magazine, "We need to keep alive the stories of Wyoming, its wildlife and the human experience of this time and place," then gave me permission to use his words that so fit the focus of my book.

Isabelle Klein, naturalist and author of *Letters from Sawdust*, long ago planted a mustard seed in my mind when she wrote, "Some day your stories will be gathered together and many more people will find themselves reading a fine book." I didn't share Isabelle's vision at the time, but she sensed a reverence for nature akin to her own. And she planted the seed.

Through the years many readers fed and watered the seed, and it sprouted and took root.

Ned, my avid outdoor man, added the nutrients, you might say, and the story grew. Many a time when he suggested, "Let's go!" I'd think, "But I really should stay home and write." After a few excursions into exciting, and sometimes treacherous places and situations, I realized he was providing the stuff that stories are made of.

I came home and wrote to my journal, my computer, my newspaper and other publications, wherever I could record my response to this fascinating place. Without Ned and his natural bonding with the out-of-doors, I might never have found the fertile ground where stories grow. I thank him for love and patience, and for his venturesome spirit that led me to the heart of Wyoming.

Appreciation and love go to my son, Gene, who repeatedly gifted me with updated electronic equipment and advice to facilitate creation of this book. Without his generosity, the stories might still reside in my head and heart.

To my friend and fellow writer, Diana Kouris, who lent unfailing support and faith, encouraged when I doubted, and shared my journey with kindness and love, thank you.

I especially appreciate the help of my sister, Lorraine Davis, who edited the manuscript with professional eye and tactful guidance, insisting that she enjoyed every minute.

Finally, I thank all the kind people who read and appreciate my writing about the Wyoming way of life. Truly, it is a land like no other in the modern world.

INTRODUCTION

"I would rather live in a world where my life is surrounded by mystery than live in a world so small that my mind could comprehend it." - Harry Emerson Fosdick

Growing up in this wild open state, I loved her rugged environment. The raw challenge teased at my spirit. But I accepted her mysteries without really seeing the unique character within. Unexposed to the world, I knew little else.

Later, my Wyoming-born husband Ned and I followed a job through Montana, Washington and finally Oklahoma, each beautiful in its own way, but more defined by development than the challenge of untamed spaces.

A trip back to Wyoming each summer took us through the high country of the Medicine Bow Forest between Fort Collins, Colorado and Laramie, Wyoming. There, despite grim warnings from city friends, we flung sleeping bags out under the stars to breathe the cool piney air and sleep to the song of coyote calls in the hills.

While I cooked breakfast next morning, cross-country truckers roared past on the nearby highway, leaning out their windows to inhale the fragrance of bacon frying over an open fire, waving and honking their horns in friendly, maybe even envious greeting.

Wyoming's wild heart called us back.

Here we found a land of startling contrast. A place where a late summer snowstorm can literally fence you in, but a January chinook may uncover flowers still in bloom beneath a blanket of insulating snow. Where a climber can disappear forever from granite peaks that snag clouds from the sky, while at their base sweet singing streams wash your cares away. Where the vastness of nature puts ego in humbling perspective, even as you whisper, "More. Tell me more. . ."

Ned has always teased that I blew into Wyoming from the Rosebud Reservation on a South Dakota tumbleweed. It's partly true. I lived a sheltered Caucasian childhood on prairie land leased from a Lakota Sioux,

Willie Runs Close to The Village. Black haired and dark eyed, I hid behind my father when Charlie Bare Heels stopped by with team and wagon to visit.

"She looks like us, Steve," Charlie said with a twinkle in his eye. "You should let us have that one."

I wasn't comfortable with Charlie's idea. But I'd gladly have wrapped myself in the beautiful, many-colored quilt Carrie White Horse made for my baby brother. Or climbed on the pinto pony to ride with handsome young Dave Star Boy.

As an adult, I lived a striking contrast to these simple lands of my youth. Residing in the more easterly corporate hometown of an international company, we flew to such cities as New York, Washington, D.C., Atlanta, Houston, and L.A., rode in limousines and stayed in fine hotels. And always, we missed our mountains.

Return to the Wind River Valley was like riding a Wyoming tumbleweed, unpredictable, daunting–yet filled with wonder. I saw Wyoming with new eyes–a place where the uncommon springs up in the midst of the ordinary, like a lovely pink bitterroot bloom brings splendor to the gray sage. The mix of nature's power and beauty, the tough-tender people, wildlife and history sang of a state less changed and defined by the world than most of North America today; of a place so sparsely populated it is said you can hear the land speak. And I heard the land say, "I have stories to tell."

I shivered with some of the trepidation that Wyoming mountain men Jim Bridger and John C. Fremont must have known in exploring uncharted territory. I leaned into the promise of this place like gold miners on old South Pass. I rode and hiked the green valleys, born of sagebrush and nursed by breasts of mountain snow. Outdoor treks revealed a heritage as ancient and mysterious as the dinosaur bones and petroglyphs recorded in the land itself. And I learned by living it, what is uncommon about Wyoming.

These are her secrets and surprises as she shared them with me.

This is Wyoming - Live -

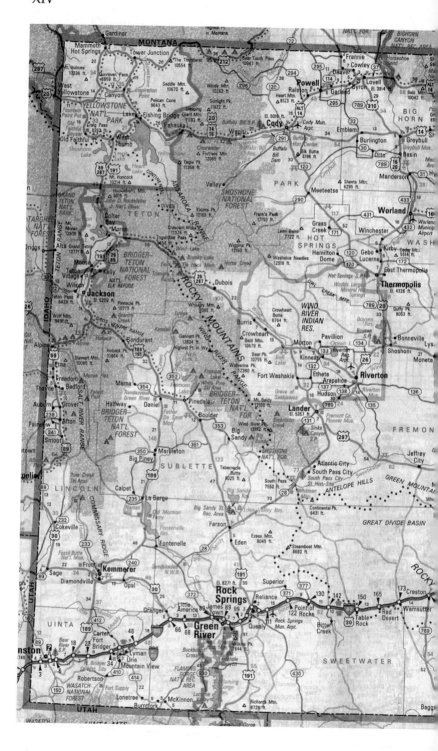

PART I

THE LAND

Surviving The Simple Life -

Life on the Wyoming land brings as many surprises as does its diverse terrain and weather. These stories depict what is often carelessly called, "the simple life." Slow lane, it is not.

HEADING FOR MOUNTAIN COUNTRY
(Trailing Double-O-Seven)

Never fear shadows. They simply mean there's a light shining nearby.
- Ruth E. Renkel

After years of living in the corporate hometown of an international company, riding in limousines and flying to cities across America, my husband Ned and I decided we might be starting to define our lives only through the man-made world we'd helped create. Though grateful for the experience, we felt a clearer, more simple reality might reveal itself in the beautiful austere high country of Wyoming, where nature proclaims her own truths and man plays by her rules. The challenge pulled like a magnet.

We'd purchased a country place in Wyoming we laughingly named Pheasant Crest Farm. We couldn't wait to get there. But first came a comedy of errors.

Our house in the state where we'd been living sold quicker than we anticipated, so we decided to store our furniture and rent a suite at the company-owned hotel for a short while. We began packing.

My mate functions like some kind of human tornado on such jobs and it's easy to get lost in the storm. One night after we'd been working for many long hours, I was in the bathroom pouring hand lotion into one bottle so I could discard the other. I turned to find the pump I'd just laid down had vanished.

"Have you seen my lotion bottle pump?"

"Isn't it on the bottle?" he asked.

"No. I laid it right here."

"Must be in the garbage I just took out."

At about 11 P.M., Ned decided to call a halt to the work for that day.

"Let's go," he said.

"Can't find my shoes," I answered.

"Don't you have them on?"

"My feet were tired. I kicked them off."

"Then they're packed."

At the swank company hotel where visiting dignitaries from the U.S. and foreign countries circulated, I sneaked in the back door in my sock feet.

The day before we moved, Ned asked me to draw money from the bank and get valuables from the safe deposit box. Instead of promptly returning to the hotel with the articles, I drove to a shopping center to pick up a layaway. Apparently I lost track of time.

On my return, I noticed a police car on a side road. Must be waiting for someone, I thought. The car moved in behind me and drove slowly along, no flashing lights, no signal to pull over. Anyway, I'm a cautious driver.

I parked behind the hotel. The police car drove up and an officer headed my way.

"What did I do?" I asked in a quivering voice.

"Nothing, ma'am. But your husband is very worried about you."

I entered the hotel and hurried to the elevator, all eyes on me. Me - The Missing One. A maid whispered, "Wow! Are you notorious! This whole place knows the story."

I slunk up to our rooms, embarrassed and remorseful about my thoughtless side-trip to the shopping center.

For years, our moves had been sponsored by "the company," but this one was on us, so we rented a U-Haul truck, feeling we could put the mover's estimate of $6,000 to better use. We started for Wyoming, Ned driving the huge rented vehicle and I our loaded pickup with camper.

Humming along behind the truck, I mused on the sign emblazoned across its rear, "ADVENTURE IN MOVING." I decided I'd better note the license number in case we got separated by traffic somewhere along the way.

Would you believe 007?

Now I knew there'd be trouble. An adventure threat backed up by the secret agent number of fiction character James Bond! What chance did I have?

We made it across Kansas and even through Denver. Nearing a large interchange east of Cheyenne, Wyoming, I pulled off the road to use pliers on the stubborn switch of my auxiliary gas tank. When I drove on, Double-O-Seven had mysteriously disappeared.

Had he taken the route through Cheyenne? Or over the hill to Laramie? My heart sank. We'd failed to discuss this interchange. After several false starts, I pulled to the side and cried.

That taken care of, my eyes cleared and I spied a gas station atop a distant hill. Maybe, just maybe, Ned had pulled that big gas hog in for a refill. Sure enough, there he was at the busy station, surrounded by a large audience for my peevish display.

He never lost sight of me the rest of the way. In fact, I believe he suggested rather firmly that I drive ahead of him.

Finally, we arrived at Pheasant Crest Farm - together. What a lovely spot! You couldn't pry me loose with a crowbar.

A LOT OF BULL

A February thaw is merely nature's way of warning us against over-optimism.
                                                          - Bill Vaughan

Not even in my wildest imaginings would I have expected to face six mean looking bulls in my front yard. Ned had left early to work on renovating the church parsonage, so I was alone on the horns of a dilemma so to speak, though the use of such a term in this case is a bit disquieting.

A chinook wind had blown all that February night, thawing long-standing snowbanks to reveal a bovine paradise - lush, tender green grass in the middle of winter. The animals smelled it from miles away and hurried to the feast. But they'd laid claim to my territory.

Annoyed, I stepped out the front door, leaving it ajar behind me. I took a few steps toward a grazing bull, assumed my most ferocious glare and yelled, "Get out of here!" The big creature lifted a horned head on a massive neck, gulped his grass, and without moving so much as a muscle, stared at me through bloodshot eyes.

I took a step backward. And another and another, easing in the door and slamming it tightly. I grabbed the phone and dialed a neighbor.

"Do you know of a herd of bulls being pastured near here?"

"Yes," she said. "On the land adjoining yours. They're rodeo stock. Don't go near them!" She provided the owner's name.

I phoned him and that afternoon a polite cowhand appeared, chased the bulls back to their pasture, then rode the fenceline to assure it wasn't down anywhere. Not wishing to perform as a rodeo clown, I remained inside all day.

The next morning I looked out the window to see my yard again occupied by a half-dozen hungry bulls. This must be a dream, I thought. It wasn't. I waited for the big critters to move away from the house a bit, then made a dash for the garage and backed the car out. Now I had refuge and weapon built into one.

I headed for the bulls and leaned on my horn. Alarmed, they turned to charge up the road toward their pasture and I rode hard on their heels enjoying the reversed roles of power. At their home fence I watched, amazed, as each raised his big body to float over a perfectly good fence as if he had wings.

At home, I phoned their owner again. No answer. I called the sheriff to inquire how I might hope to safely step out into my own yard. A kindly sounding deputy assured me they'd take action if the threatening situation continued.

"Keep in touch," he said.

That afternoon, I looked out to see a big red bull in my front yard. I opened the door and yelled, "Scram!"

He lifted his head, blew a snort of dust at me and glared. I backed into my house and called the sheriff's office. The next morning, a deputy phoned me.

"You'll see the owner of the rodeo stock arriving shortly with a cattle truck to remove the bulls from your area," he said. "Apparently such animals can't be contained by ordinary fences."

Apparently.

On schedule, the truck appeared and the critters were loaded. My gratitude was boundless. I'd never called a sheriff for assistance before. I was impressed with the prompt and reliable help provided. Later, we were to learn how quickly three deputies and an ambulance can arrive when a drunk man beat on our door in the middle of the night to announce, "Dead man down the road!"

But that's another story of life in Wyoming at the place we originally thought we'd name "Slow Lane." Somehow, it doesn't seem that would ever have been appropriate.

DEAD MAN DOWN THE ROAD

Normal day, let me be aware of the treasure you are.
- Mary Jean Irion

About 12:30 one cold Saturday night, we were awakened by an insistent pounding on our back door. We yanked on clothes enough to be decent and moved cautiously through the house, I quivering along behind Ned, trying to decide what to grab for a weapon if needed.

Ned opened the door slowly and called, "Got a problem?"

"Yeah," came the answer. "Dead man down the road. Call the sherff." The man's speech was slurred. He was drunk. Or pretending to be.

"How did he die?" Ned asked. "Someone kill him?"

"Yeah. Me an' 'nother guy beat him. Call the sherff."

The night was bitterly cold. The man, wearing only a light jacket and no cap had walked a good half-mile from the old trailer where neighbors once housed transient farm help.

Ned eyed the man's pockets for concealed weapons, then said, "OK. Come inside while I phone. But sit on that bench by the door. If you try anything, you'll be out in the cold before you know what happened."

"Yessir. Yessir," said the man, as polite as he was drunk.

Ned dialed the sheriff from the phone near where the man sat, keeping an eye on him all the while. "Better make coffee," he said to me with a nod toward the man. "He can use it."

The sheriff's office answered at once. "Stay on the line until we get a deputy there so we'll know you're OK," said the dispatcher.

I handed the inebriated man a mug of strong, hot coffee. "Thankew ma'am, thankew," came the courteous response as he wrapped both hands around the warm mug.

Within 15 minutes our country road, a full 17 miles from town, was alive with more flashing lights than a Christmas tree. Two deputies and an ambulance headed for the trailer, while a third officer wheeled into our yard.

Before the deputy could ask, our visitor rose to his feet and leaned spread-eagled against the wall. A smile flitted across Ned's face as he glanced my way. The man knew the procedure well.

The deputy arrived from the trailer. "The guy isn't dead," he reported. "He's unconscious, badly beaten. The ambulance will tend him."

The two deputies frisked the drunk and led him to their car.

"Thanks fer yer hosp-talty," he mumbled politely as he left.

We closed the door and burst into laughter. One week later, the man was back, rapping at our door in the cold, early dawn. Suddenly, it wasn't so funny again.

"Seen my wife, sir-rr?" the man asked. "Can't find 'er."

"No," said Ned in a tone of disgust as he closed the door.

"I don't care where she is," he told me. Then he put on his coat and went out to hunt for her, just like I knew he would.

He didn't find her. For a while we worried about the woman, but we needn't have. She was back at the trailer wondering where her errant husband had gone.

Eventually, the rowdy bunch knocked the big windows out of the trailer and the brawls ended. The cure seemed so simple now - just a bit of winter air-conditioning to cool the enthusiasm . . .

Brandy and baby Mick at Pheasant Crest Farm.

Ned Case photo

POWER OF MOTHERHOOD

In the face of uncertainty, there is nothing wrong with hope.
- Bernie Siegel

Motherhood in the animal world can be as interesting and challenging as in our own, and in many ways more difficult to deal with. Probably because they know some things we don't.

Ned and I were both raised in the country, but we'd never owned a horse until Brandy, a high-strung, buckskin-colored quarterhorse mare came to live with us at Pheasant Crest Farm. We had a lot to learn.

On a chilly late April morning, we checked Brandy from every angle as she struggled to give birth. "Are you sure she's alright?" I asked every few minutes, anxious and almost feeling the contractions myself.

Brandy lay down, stood up, tried every position. Time dragged on and we worried and stewed. Finally Mick was born about 11:00 A.M.

The dun-colored stud colt with black mane and tail arrived in a temperature of less than 40 degrees, an icy wind blowing out of the north. Ned rubbed the shivering Mick with burlap bags while I held a horse blanket to shield them from the wind.

Wearing coveralls about the color of Brandy and by now smelling much like Mick himself, Ned soon discovered the colt was nuzzling and bonding with him instead of Brandy.

Now Brandy's mothering instinct came on strong. Not to be eliminated from this process, she hovered nervously, then lay down and rolled in the afterbirth, apparently knowing if she was to win this case she'd have to wear the strong body scent her baby would recognize. Ned pushed Mick to his mother's side and soon the two were nickering softly as Brandy pulled Mick close with her nose to nurse at the colostrum-laced milk he must have to survive. We moved away, happy to let Brandy take over.

Brandy's once sleek form now looked badly misshapen, the muscles on the sides of her belly hanging loose and bulging. But Brandy knew just how to deal with her figure problem. She lay down on bare ground and with great vigor and purpose rolled this way and that, this way and that. When at last she stood, we could hardly believe our eyes.

The muscles were all back in place. In just minutes, Brandy had become slim and sleek as before her pregnancy.

That night, a snowstorm blew in and fell wet and heavy until midnight. We hadn't built a barn yet and fearing for the safety of the new colt, Ned put him in a small shed and fastened a sturdy wooden panel in the door so Brandy and her babe could see, smell and touch one another.

When Ned went to check on them later, he found Mick outside with his mother, the panel still firmly in place. How in the world did she get him over it?

Next morning as Ned approached the corral, Brandy, who usually welcomed, even sought his attention, took one suspicious look and headed for the open gate. With Mick at her side they raced, manes and tails riding the wind to the far end of the farm. In Brandy's world the message was clear: You have to fight for your offspring. First that bonding thing, then the shed.

Ned coaxed her back with a gallon of oats and a peck of apologies.

Mick fast became our pet. Curious and amusing, he wanted to be a part of everything we did. When Ned put him and his mother out to feed on the grass, Mick ran to the plowed garden spot to buck and tear around in the warm soil. Soon he began to sample the strawberry plants and a little grass, lying down right in the middle of the garden for a nap in the sun.

When Ned began placing the saddle on Brandy again each morning, little Mick backed off and stared. He snorted, bucked, then sulked off to the corral, refusing to follow such a weird, humpbacked parent. Eventually, Mick discovered he could miss the morning trek up the rocky ridge where fox kits played in the sand. Now he followed his saddled mother.

When Mick was grown, Lady, a morgan-quarter-horse breed, came to Pheasant Crest and gave birth. Brandy, not even pregnant now, quickly fell into the maternity mode again. She moved in boldly to clean Lady's colt, tried to nurse it with no milk in store for the job, and in fact, attempted outright kidnap. She lost, but not because she didn't try.

Never underestimate the power and potential of motherhood.

HELEN MARIAH

To understand any living thing, you must, so to say, creep within and feel the beating of its heart. - W. MacNeile Dixon

Helen Mariah visited her doctor the other day. It was Sunday and it was early, but Dr. Jim met her at his office in a pleasant mood and gently called her "baby" as he examined her sick little body. You can tell he loves his patients.

Helen Mariah is a very plain looking little calico cat. But like anyone worth knowing, she has great depth and mystery. Her very name might seem an enigma to some. It does have rhyme and reason, however. It came out of my own past.

My father didn't use profanity, at least not around his wife and daughters. After we grew up and he figured he'd taught us all the good stuff he knew, he relaxed his self-discipline a bit. A moment of exasperation in those years might be expressed by a low growled, "Well, Helen Mariah!" (Accent on the first syllable of Helen.) Then his eyes would roll slyly to see if anyone had noticed this bold departure from his self-imposed rule.

Based on that story, Helen Mariah might seem misnamed. There's certainly nothing profane about this gentle, ladylike kitty. But I can explain.

You see, we bought Pheasant Crest Farm from my parents and a sense of their presence seems to linger. It's in the air. In fact, my dad's wry experiment with profanity was floating around here the day I tripped over the cat and fell headlong into an irrigation ditch.

"Well, Helen Mariah!" were the first words that came out of my mouth. (Accent on the first syllable of Helen, of course.)

When I recovered from the injuries of my fall, I shortened the cat's name to Mariah, the haunting notes of the beautiful song, "They Call The Wind Mariah," echoing through the back rooms of my mind. It's a name easy for her to pronounce, too.

To Ned, Mariah's not nearly so complicated, either in name or character. She's simply "Putty Cat," and she trots around after him to feed the horses in winter or make garden in summer. If there's snow on the ground, she may hitch a ride on his arm.

But I've seen her stalk the berry patch as if some mysterious creature might lurk there. Then suddenly, she attacks a strawberry plant and mauls it like a leopard after a springbok. Our berries are jam before we pick them.

When I gather green beans and peas, she grabs them out of my pan and tastes them, then looks into my eyes with a questioning meow as if to say, "How can you eat this junk?"

Mariah is an outdoor cat, but firmly convinced she's miscast in that role. In fact, she puts great effort into proving what a compatible full-time guest she'd be if allowed inside.

Once she slipped into the house unnoticed as we left on a four-day trip and spent the time imprisoned. She survived by eating one house plant and drinking from a bathroom stool.

She even knew what a bathroom is for. She pulled a brown bath mat off the tub, did what comes naturally, then folded in all four corners of the mat to conceal it. Nowhere in the house did she leave any kind of problem.

There's one phase of domesticity Mariah violently dislikes, though. She views a car ride as next to intolerable, wailing pitifully when she looks out the window and sees the world racing by. I sympathize. Sometimes the world zips past me, too. It's a time for wailing.

At home, according to Doctor Jim's directions, we gave Mariah a round of antibiotics and a baby vitamin. We learned a few things in the process. One is that it's smarter to buy this expensive vitamin in pill form. The pill may eventually (I think) get pushed down her throat. I foolishly believed the liquid might go down easier. Ned and I and Mariah all ended up drenched in the foul smelling vitamin as she gargled and spewed it in all directions. Though quite ill, she promptly began to bathe and didn't stop until all the offensive stuff was off her coat.

Mariah is well now, but I'm still remembering the shot Dr. Jim gave her that first day. She brightened and frolicked around here for an hour or so as if she'd just downed a fifth of catnip tea.

If my own doctor doesn't start treating me better, I may go see Dr. Jim.

MODERN DAY SHEEPHERDER

The truth of the matter is you always know the right thing to do.
The hard part is doing it.   *-Gen. H. Norman Schwarzkopf*

It was 5:30 on a cold January morning when the blond young woman in jeans and Levi jacket knocked at our door.

"I need to call the sheriff," she said, looking shaken but determined. "Can I use your phone? I just shot someone's dog. It had my sheep piled up down by the water hole."

We'd leased our winter pasture to her father a couple of days earlier. Just yesterday, she'd found 18 handsome yearling lambs dead near the hole where year-round water flowed. She called her father.

The irate rancher seeking a suspect roared into our yard. Apparently noting we had no livestock except two saddle horses and a couple of cats, he decided the horses were most likely to have attacked his flock. He opened his pickup door and hit the ground stomping and shouting.

Ned was caught completely off guard. But the obscenities and vile accusations riled him.

"Knock it off, mister," he ordered. "I don't like that kind of talk. And this is my property you're standing on."

The rancher looked surprised. The shouting wound down. He stared at his dusty old boots as if he couldn't believe they'd taken him to this vulnerable spot.

"I apologize," he said, finally, yanking his hat down over his eyes. "I was upset."

"OK," said Ned, "Now shall we try to figure out what happened?"

They talked. We'd noticed a gray dog running through our yard the day before. We didn't know who it belonged to. We didn't believe our horses would attack sheep, but corralled them, anyway. They were still there when the girl arrived to say she'd killed a gray dog.

"I just drove up, shone the headlights of my pickup on it and shot it with my .38 revolver," she said.

The girl had a fresh outdoor look and a strange little hillbilly accent. But this was no backwoods woman. She knew her rights, the law, and exactly how to proceed. She phoned the sheriff's deputy, then asked Ned to accompany her to the water hole to witness the sheep and the dog.

By the time the deputy arrived, I had coffee, buttermilk pancakes, sausage and eggs on the table. Why? I don't know. Nerve tonic, maybe. The girl ate, confident but quiet. The rotund deputy joked as he downed the meal that he'd "surely responded to the right call this time."

By now, they'd decided the dog most likely belonged to our neighbor. The deputy and the girl drove to inform him that not only had his loved pet been killed, but he would be liable for 18 dead sheep as well.

Though we had no legal involvement in this sad event, Ned and I felt compassion for both sides. When the old rancher drove through our yard, the dead yearlings piled high on his pickup truck, I truly felt nauseous.

We went to tell our neighbor how sorry we were about their loved pet, how we hated having it killed on our place.

"It wasn't your fault," he said with tear-filled eyes. "But it's hard. The kids cried all weekend." Everyone knew the dog shouldn't have run loose. We shared our tears, nonetheless.

In the end the sheep were again left without someone to tend them. The rancher's daughter herself had commented, "Of course, they're never safe without a herder." Then she, her father and two ranch hands all climbed into their vehicle and drove away.

WET WEEDS WON'T BURN

I couldn't wait for success . . . so I went ahead without it.
- Jonathan Winters

"Can you come and man the water hose while I burn weeds?" my mate called in the door one early spring morning.

"Can I what?" I asked.

"Man the hose." He headed for the tool shed.

I smiled. It's a little hard to imagine a 5'1", 115 pound female manning anything. Maybe I could woman it though. I hoped he was prepared for the substitution.

Out behind the house, Ned pressurized his weed burner and lit a match. The weeds and leaves in the deep irrigation lateral burst into crackling orange and yellow flames.

"Now, don't let it cross the ditch," he warned.

While I was still wondering why the spray nozzle wasn't on the hose straight and water was shooting all over my jeans and boots, he shouted, "It's across the ditch!"

He snatched the hose from my hand, leaped to the other side and extinguished the fire. That taken care of, I resumed my position as chief fireman - er, firewoman.

The weeds burst into flame again. Smoke billowed, burning my eyes and throat. How was I supposed to see if fire had crossed the ditch when I couldn't even keep my eyes open? I squinted and shot a healthy spray of water through the smoke just in case.

"Wet weeds won't burn," Ned observed.

Apparently, I'd miscalculated the distance. So what's new? That's the same ditch where I met personal disaster a couple of years ago when I misguessed my ability to jump it.

I did grow a bit more adept at my job as work

progressed. But climbing over fallen branches doesn't bring out the grace in me, especially when I'm trying to pull 100 feet of garden hose behind. Before long, I'd caught the toe of my boot, staggered and stumbled.

"Hey! Watch what you're doing!" I heard from below.

I looked over my shoulder to see I'd watered down both Ned and the fire he was struggling to keep alive in the ditch.

He set down his burner and came to untangle the hose from the brush and get me back on track. A breeze rose from the east and flames began to shoot down the bank at a lively pace. It was time to spring to duty.

Again, the hose refused to cooperate. This time, part of it hung in a small tree. The remainder coiled around me like a boa constrictor. Ned hurried to my aid and gave the hose a yank, nearly flipping me into the next county.

By 4:30, the ditch was clean and black. Ned and I were dirty and black. And soaked from our boots to the seat of our jeans. One thing for sure, there'd been no danger either of us would catch fire. My performance had tended to that.

As we headed for the house, a bath and dry clothes, Ned commented, "Well, we got that job done."

"We," he said.

I wondered if it had occurred to him how much faster and easier he might have done it without me.

In the distance, a fire siren wailed.

"Someone's spring burn must be out of control," he said.

"Probably didn't have a woman manning the hose," I added, suddenly feeling a little smug.

We hadn't, after all, had to call the fire department.

TREES: THINGS TO BE TREASURED

If you would know strength and patience, welcome the company of trees.   *- Hal Borland*

Trees on irrigated Wyoming lands are something to be treasured. The giant leafy guardians towering above our house and yard are probably 50 years old, having been planted in the 1930s. We're glad the original owners helped so many get started back then.

Trees have been memorable to me since I was four. A big one in my grandparents' front yard beckoned one day and Mother caught the faraway look in my eye.

"Now don't climb up there," she said. "You'll fall."

When she went into the house, the tree called again and I climbed it. Sure enough, I fell. On my head. I reveled in the attention that followed, remembering to this day being carried to a bed in my uncle's room, one that was always off limits before. Mother and Grandma hovered over me for an hour or so, whispering and watching.

Recalling the event now, I wonder if the head landing might have slipped a synapse in my brain. Soon after that, I started trying to write. Were he living today, Grandpa would likely insist the tendency was inherited, having been a newspaper publisher himself. But on the days when my creative senses elude me, I wonder about the tree in his yard that grabbed me, like the one that snatched "Peanuts" cartoon character Charlie Brown and his kite each spring.

For one thing, ever since that day I've viewed the woody perennials as semi-human, almost to the point that it pains me to see them pruned. Common horticultural sense tells me they might grow more beautiful if they underwent reconstructive surgery, but then so might one's nose.

So what if a tree has two legs when it should have one, and arms that grow out of its hips? A pair of beautiful orioles doesn't mind, so long as the tree stands sturdy enough to allow a safe nest in her hair.

Some call the arborescent growths a nuisance. They do require a little in return for the pleasure they give, but not much. An occasional drink until they reach puberty, perhaps. Then they fend for themselves, exploring the deep earth for most of their needs. In summer, they thank us by extending cool, leafy limbs for shade when days grow hot and long.

Granted, most do rather brazenly drop their garments in fall, but how else could the winter sun filter into our house when it's cold outside? Most people view that strip act as a tease situation requiring vigorous response with a rake, but it's possible the trees are just attempting to keep their feet warm. After all, isn't that where their hearts reside in winter? It wouldn't bother me to just leave the leaves in thoughtful reciprocation for the sunshine they allow me for warmth.

In general, I'm quite defensive of trees. I've learned that where a tree is provided, a bird will visit, and where birds visit our garden is free of bugs. Besides the great horned owls who hatched two chicks each spring, we've seen nesting robins, kingbirds, larks, swallows, orioles, tanagers, finches, flickers and chickadees at our Wyoming country home. What a glorious variety of color and song.

Today, most of us take for granted the trees' friendly presence in this once sagebrushed area. Yet, except for those that haunt the river's edge, few grew here in the early 1930s. The lovely oases that exist on the farmsteads now were created by stubborn pioneer men and women who deeply valued their windbreak, beauty and shade-giving properties.

Recognizing that trees, like humans and all living things do age and die, Ned plants two or three every year or so. We hope others are doing the same.

And as for my slipped synapse, Charlie Brown exaggerates. It's kind of nice to be grabbed by a tree.

CONFUSION IN THE ANIMAL WORLD

We are never prepared for what we expect
                                                    - James A. Michener

The farmhouse at Pheasant Crest overflowed with family visitors the morning Mystie was born. She received a rousing human welcome but met the animal world in fear and confusion.

"Did you know that Lady has a new colt?" asked my sister on return from an early walk. "That's not all," she added. "The other mare, Brandy, has kidnapped it."

"No, I didn't know!" Ned charged out the door.

Lady wasn't supposed to be pregnant and showed almost no visible signs of impending birth. Nevertheless, Mystie (short for mystery) had arrived, a healthy, petite charcoal-colored filly.

Shortly, the big house came alive with shouts, bare feet pounding the stairs and humans racing half-dressed to the corrals to view the equine miracle. But the phenomena had only begun.

While Brandy, the kidnapper, worked enthusiastically at bathing Lady's new babe and made every effort to nurse her with no milk in store for the job, Lady stood in the distance, a nonchalant observer of all the commotion.

Knowing Mystie must receive her mother's colostrum-laced milk to survive, Ned tied Lady in a stall and distracted her with hay cubes every two hours while her offspring suckled. Bottle feedings filled in the spaces.

In the meantime, Brandy, craving even surrogate motherhood, snorted, whinnied and pawed ground across the fence. But Mystie seemed to know Lady should nurture her, despite all the confusion. The poor little creature stood forlornly pleading for acceptance and sustenance, perhaps even simple adoption if Lady could drum up nothing else. All Mystie got was a swift kick in the side when she ventured near.

After three days, Ned grew discouraged. "Call the neighbors and see if their kids want a colt to bottle feed," he said.

Lady must have heard the discussion. As soon as I made the phone call she reached out her nose, sniffed at Mystie and began to nuzzle her lovingly. Assuming an inviting nursing pose with hind leg drawn back and relaxed, she pulled Mystie close with her nose, urging her to suckle.

The colt hesitated. Was this some kind of trick? Lady continued to shower her babe with maternal affection, almost running the bonding thing into the ground. Embarrassed, I phoned the neighbor.

"I hope you haven't - told your children - about the colt yet." I stammered. "Apparently Lady's hormones are back to normal."

Before long Mystie began to trust her mother and Brandy gradually backed off as Lady assumed the dominant role.

Mystie is a handsome, graceful 18-month-old filly now with a gentle nature. She wears the bridle and she and Ned go for a spirited leading lesson each day. Yet I wonder if her uncertain beginnings still haunt her.

We thought she was weaned, but recently when something frightened her, she went through a strange performance of trying to nurse again. Of course, Lady no longer had milk. Still, Mystie would take a bite of grass then reach for a couple of pulls at the dry udder, another bite of grass, another hopeful suck. This peculiar performance continued until finally Lady walked away in disgust.

Today, I wonder. Might the colt, like a once-rejected child, still deal with recurring insecurities? Or did she just recall where she'd left the nectar that might make dry autumn forage more palatable?

SKIING AN ALFALFA FIELD

We do not take a trip; a trip takes us   *- John Steinbeck*

If I'd taken up with a less venturesome man I'd probably be wintering in Arizona instead of returning to outdoor sports at this age. Though I've announced repeatedly that I'm not a sportswoman, I've been talked into rafting the Yellowstone River in Montana, the Illinois in Oklahoma, and the Yakima in Washington. There were climbs up Montana's Hell Roaring Mountain, Grasshopper Glacier and others, each a full story event in its own right.

I didn't handle all these excursions with the utmost grace and good will, of course, but I must admit life hasn't been dull. And the surprises aren't over. Who'd ever think of skiing an alfalfa field?

One winter morning at Pheasant Crest Farm Ned awoke to discover that dry brown stubble had been transformed into a beautiful ski-scape. Most people just thought it snowed. "Besides," he said, "The skies are blue and the air is fresh and invigorating."

We dashed off to town for ski equipment.

I must confess there's something sensual about new powder snow. The feeling comes right up through the skis, through those wool socks and heavy boots. I can't explain it, but I'm convinced this awareness places me in some category of advancement as a skier.

We were quite unprepared, though, for the response of the resident community at Pheasant Crest to our ski equipment. The elm tree owls with whom we share a reciprocal staring relationship, took one wide-eyed look at us and flapped off across the field to the neighbor's trees.

Mariah, the cat, sniffed us cautiously. When she concluded our toes had grown to disproportionate length, her ears lay back in disapproval, as though we'd been caught in a lie and the Pinocchio syndrome had been misdirected. Eventually, she seemed to realize it was all for fun and began making her own little snowballs to toss in the air as she frolicked in our tracks.

When we entered the field, the wary horses approached with a wild glint in their eyes. They snorted loudly and circled us in great suspicion, their sensitive noses extended as if our aberrant behavior might be analyzed by a scent that matched it. Then they backed off, snorted and advanced to reconsider our abnormalities.

Mystie, the colt, who is forever trying to stir the mares into frisky activity, finally decided we weren't as weird as she'd first suspected and nearly got on the skis with us.

A neighbor riding the range to check his cattle stopped and sat his horse stiffly as he stared out across the land in our direction.

"Maybe he thinks we're a pair of fleetfooted deer skimming the fields," I suggested.

"And maybe your imagination is over-stimulated by the brisk exercise," observed Ned.

A buck and eight does standing tightly bunched on a nearby ditch bank weren't fooled. Long ears stood at alert from every direction, like twigs on a grove of trees. When we skied near, the deer broke from standstill to a bounce that lifted them several feet in the air. A bounding rhythm took them quickly across the sagebrush and out of sight behind a distant ridge.

By the end of the second day, ligaments in my legs screamed their objection to further activity and I barely made it in to the couch.

Thinking back, I've concluded it's actually a blessing that I'm coaxed into the outdoor life in spite of myself. The surprises are fun, the skies are blue and the air fresh and invigorating. And maybe the wild creatures and the neighbors can stand a little amazement. After all, who ever heard of skiing an alfalfa field?

BUILD IT YOURSELF–AND LAUGH

Progress is man's ability to complicate simplicity.
                                        - *Thor Heyerdahl*

I received a beautiful cedar chest for Christmas. It was shipped to Wyoming all the way from the Ozarks, cut, grooved and marked for assembly. On the front page of the owner's manual of the Oz Cedar Chest #615, its manufacturer turned on the humor.

"Welcome to the Land of Oz. We have designed your cedar chest so even a scarecrow can follow our simple instructions...and have fun putting it together."

A couple of men who must remain anonymous (and you'll soon see why) decided to assemble the colorful, aromatic chest in the middle of the living room at Pheasant Crest Farm. Sketches accompanied each consecutively numbered instruction, couched in words any scarecrow could comprehend, even before the wizard endowed him with a brain: "Get hammer; get screws and screwdriver; get nut; put nut on bolt," etc. With specifics like this, how can we miss?

Soon the bottom, sides and ends are installed in the grooves. Everything fits. Now we're down to Instruction No. 6: Installing lid and lock.

I wonder why I need a lock on this piece of furniture. It's not a safe. Do moths invade unlocked cedar chests?

The workmen install the lock, cautiously making sure the key is outside the chest. The lid is lowered. Click.

It's time to try it out. Does it open? No. the key is inserted in the lock, rattling and quivering in a nervous hand. The lock does not release.

"Here. Let me try it."

"OK. Maybe I didn't do it right."

From another room where it had seemed best to seclude myself, I hear someone clearing his throat. A nervous cough. A few guttural expletives. Finally, I decide to go check on my little cedar chest.

As I enter the room, the men rock back on their heels in laughter. "It's locked. The key won't open it."

"This is a humorous situation?" I ask. "Or simply a state of advanced hysteria?"

The men turn suddenly sober. "Don't worry. We'll just remove the hinges from the back of the lid."

Done. But the lock maintains its stubborn grasp. A man's hand gripping a screwdriver reaches in from the back, scraping skin as it strains to undo the screws from the lock part inside the front of the chest.

I hold my breath as I check the owner's manual. "You may notice some surface cracks in the wood," it reads. "This is natural to sturdy native Ozark cedar."

But how sturdy is the cedar? The creaking sounds I'm hearing hint that we might soon notice more than surface cracks.

At last the lid is off, with lock still firmly attached.

One of the craftsmen now decides to check the easy-to-follow directions. His eyes grow bright, as if the wizard has suddenly granted him knowledge.

"Does something on the front page of this instruction sheet just sort of jump out at you?" he asks, handing it to his fellow workman.

There in large red print that clearly does jump out from the black are the words, "PUSH BUTTON LOCK."

One of the men pushes the lock. It pops open.

"I think I feel a story coming on," I announce as they re-install the hinged lid to the chest. "People should hear how following simple directions can lead to success. Saves getting lost on the yellow brick road."

This world is full of intrepid writers, but they'll never know real fear until they're pursued by a couple of enlightened scarecrows threatening mayhem if their story shows up in print. So in order to save my own neck, I may have to make one slight confession.

I didn't see the large red print either.

TRACTOR TALES

It is the unknown with all its disappointments and surprises that is the most interesting. — Anne Morrow Lindbergh

I heard a nostalgic spring sound one April morning at Pheasant Crest and looked out to see my beaming mate aboard the humming old Ford tractor. Apparently, I thought, the little blue machine has agreed to serve one more season.

Watching the two of them chug down the lane together, I wondered if tractors might grow to be more than mechanical things, perhaps in years of companionship with man becoming some kind of storehouse of philosophy or wisdom. Some pretty heavy stuff is laid on them out there in the fields. Who else besides God and the birds could one talk to those endless days?

No doubt tractors catch more profanity than is their due, but I suspect they also share a man's dreams, frustrations and prayers. There's a lot to absorb.

My father's old John Deere must have been saturated with philosophy. Clearly, it imparted wisdom to him from time to time. He had only to consult its "innards" to find the answer to a problem. One case in particular impressed me.

When I was sixteen, we moved to Wyoming from South Dakota, where I fell in love with a schoolmate a year older than I. He gave me a beautiful gold-filled locket ordered from Montgomery Ward. A week later he mailed me a letter.

"I'm not coming to see you again," he wrote. "In plain words, you sort of get in my blood. Anyway, I have no faith in marriage."

I was devastated. "Plain words! What does it mean, I get in his blood?" I wailed.

Though my father preferred to shy away from emotional encounters, his automatic response to challenge, including my teenage love affairs, continually led him into them.

"Means - he thinks - maybe - he loves you," he blurted.

"But he said he wasn't coming back!" I cried.

I clutched the locket to my breast and wept for days.

Finally, one morning Daddy called, "Come help me repair the tractor. I need you to hand me the wrenches."

Beside the old John Deere out by the shed, Daddy tinkered away for what seemed an hour. Nothing much appeared to be happening except for a running stream of pleasant, pointless conversation on his part. I stood by the big toolbox, waiting. He didn't seem to be needing the wrenches. I wondered when he would.

At last Daddy cleared his throat. From the bowels of the old tractor where his voice sounded like he was consulting the carburetor, I heard, "About that letter from your boyfriend. When he's old enough, if he really loves you, nothing in this world could convince him you couldn't have a happy marriage. Remember that. Now put on a smile and go out with the other boys who ask you."

The tractor repair apparently completed, I was dismissed to go help Mother prepare lunch.

A few years later, the young man whose blood I'd invaded asked me to share his life, absolutely certain the future was invented just for us.

Many years have passed and the locket still gleams, intact and treasured, along with the marriage. The man I watched chug down the lane on his little blue Ford tractor this morning is the very one who said he couldn't marry me because in plain words, "You sort of get in my blood." I understand the term better now. I hope he's never cured.

And old tractors? I'll bet they could tell more about human nature than mechanical power. They probably should be revered in museums. Some are there, of course, but as worn-out relics of a mechanized world. If we'd listen with our hearts, they might reveal poignant tales of real lives. Like the stories we hear from old saddles and guns.

POLLY DEALS WITH SUMMER SNOW

Some things have to be believed to be seen.   - *Ralph Hodgson*

When nature went berserk in Fremont county, Wyoming on the night of Monday, September 13, the local newspaper called the event a "late summer snowstorm." But Garfield, the comic strip cat, perceptively covered his head and swore he wouldn't even get up on Monday, the 13th.

Not knowing how to respond to Garfield's shrewd observation, I was sadly unprepared for what happened and that night more than ready to open my home to Polly, a mysterious pioneer woman more familiar with basic survival techniques than I.

About 6 P.M., snow began falling at our tranquil rural home, soft and beautiful and most unseasonal. As night fell, so did more snow, thick and fast and heavy laden with moisture. The huge canopy of 80 to 90 foot cottonwood and elm trees surrounding our house and 3-acre yard grew even more picturesque in their fresh fluffy draping.

"It's a fairyland," I murmured as we took one last peek through the lace curtains before climbing into bed.

We'd barely closed our eyes when we were jolted erect by a resounding crash to one side of our room, then a crack, followed by a smashing roar to the other side.

"What in the world is happening?" I gasped.

"D-don't know," Ned stuttered.

We leaped to the windows and stared. In the eerie white radiance of the security light out by the garage a scene of horror grew. All about us great tree limbs began to creak, shudder, then crash to the ground, sprawling like quivering giants across the big yard. Not old dead skeletons, but enormous green branches, still vibrant and heavy with leaves on this not yet autumn night.

Swiftly, Ned yanked on jeans, jacket and boots and headed for the back door, my frantic protests trailing behind him.

"Don't go!" I pleaded. "It's disaster out there!"

"I have to!" He dashed into the moaning night.

"Come back!" I called. "Please come back!

"But the new travel trailer . . . I have to move it . . . to the clearing!" His words bounced back erratically as if ricocheted off the tumbling trees.

I pushed the door shut against the storm and ran to throw open a window. The keening of wounded trees echoed through the night like soldiers crying out to one another in disarray and defeat as they fell to Earth.

"Forget the trailer!" I screamed out the window. "I need you. If a tree falls on you, I can't get it off. It could break your back, kill you. The driveway's a jungle. We're trapped."

Unhearing or unheeding, Ned sped into the darkness and my words floated off to join the vain arboreal cries that rent the air.

Desperation seized me. Not only had nature gone mad, but Ned's good sense appeared to have deserted him as well. Powerless, frightened and near hysteria, I fell into great gasping sobs, holding my body in my own trembling arms.

Shortly, I felt a strange presence, a movement of air beside me. Or was it?

Struggling to see through my tears, I sensed more than saw the strong woman who said in a calm voice, "Settle down. We can handle this."

That's when I thought she slipped in the back way.

Glancing toward the window, I heard a mumble, "Who needs a confounded second home, anyway?"

The voice softened as she turned. "My, what a nice little wood stove, so warm and comforting."

Still rubbing my eyes, I followed the strange presence into the bathroom where she pulled damp disheveled hair neatly back from her face and pinned it at the sides with small brown combs. Then, almost as if speaking to her own reflection in the mirror, she announced, "Name's Polly. I'm here to help. Let's have at it."

"Summer Snow" brings trauma to trees and travel trailer.

Ned Case photo

"Summer Snow" pulls huge tree limbs to the house roof and yard at Pheasant Crest Farm.

Ned Case photo

Looking the picture of a true "early settler" now, Polly took command, issuing clipped orders which I questioned only occasionally. Such willing acquiescence was quite out of character for me, but this Polly person was clearly more adept at coping than I.

Back in the kitchen, Polly knelt and dug a sunny little teakettle from the dark reaches of my cabinets, filled its yellow belly with water and set it on the wood stove in the den. Soon it burst into merry song, a heartwarming symbol of light and hope. Outside, pandemonium reigned.

I hovered near a window, trying to keep Ned in sight. Like a puppet on a string, he floundered, pulled this way then that. He started the pickup truck, then promptly became mired in snow, mud and fallen timber. Mounting the old Ford tractor, only seconds passed before he recognized his vulnerability and ran for the safety of the garage.

After what seemed eternity, Ned moved into view again. In the rays of the security light, I watched him start for the house, lift his head to search the treetops for danger, then shake it in despair as he noted the chaos about him. Hugging the buildings for protection, he tripped and stumbled through huge soggy limbs, while others continued to creak, crack, then land in a shower of snow on the outbuildings and carpet the spaces between. At last, he neared the house.

"Thank God, you're back!" I cried, pulling him in the door. A monstrous limb fell to close off the trail, its leaves slapping at his heels.

"Wind's coming up." Apprehension filled Ned's voice as he rubbed his cold hands and brushed at his snow-plastered jeans. "Could blow some of the snow off the trees. Still, they're so weighted. . ."

Soon we heard the ominous sound of the rising wind tugging at more and bigger branches. A resounding crack and a blinding flash of light sent us whirling to the windows.

"Oh, no - not the garage!" Ned moaned. The entire side of the building glowed with blue sparks exploding wildly in all directions as a weary bough broke loose and sprawled across electric wires, ripping them from the garage and carrying them live into a foot of wet snow.

I groped for Ned in the dark.

Polly, bless her, already had a fat gold candle and "strike anywhere" matches set out on the television.

"Just as well get some use out of that worthless piece of furniture," she'd mumbled earlier as she prepared for rural electric to give up the ghost, an event she saw as imminent.

Sure enough, now even the security light, independent of other REA power, blinked out. Total darkness sucked in the countryside and isolation was complete.

Polly, with a knowing air, calmly lit the candle. She hurried to the kitchen and returned carrying a tray.

"Fresh cinnamon rolls?" she asked with a smugness I saw as a little absurd. I had, after all, lifted those very rolls warm and fragrant from my self-cleaning electric oven earlier in the day. Polly served them now with milk in the glow of the gold candle as proudly as if she'd labored over them for hours. We huddled near the homey wood stove and consoled ourselves with the sweet spicy pastry through the long night.

How I yearned for light. Daylight. Would it never come? I listened to the grandfather clock making its melodic announcements of time, and waited.

"Soothing," Polly mused. Then she added dryly, "One more thing beside the candle and wood stove that can function on its own."

Next day, Ned threw the electrical breaker switch and clambered out through the greenwood graveyard to drag huge limbs from the top of our house and outbuildings. Polly whipped around, sloshing through snowbanks and branches to gather wood from the pile out by the garage.

Of course, Ned had cut and hauled the firewood from the mountains a week ago. But Polly carried in one armload after another as nobly as if she'd searched the forest for it stick by stick. I appreciated her courageous spirit, though she did seem a bit over-zealous at times.

Now we brought in buckets of moisture-filled snow, dumping it into large containers about the kitchen.

"Never know when we might need every drop we can get," Polly observed. "Electric well pump could be off for days out here. Have to depend on yourself and what nature sets out for you."

Toward noon, Polly pulled a now-thawed chicken from the solemn refrigerator and began to cut it up.

"*How* are we going to cook that?" I wondered aloud.

"Simple," came her quick response. "Let it simmer on the wood stove in a frying pan. Be delicious."

"Frying pan?"

"Sure. Large flat bottom grabs more heat." Polly slapped on the lid.

Next she peeled potatoes and placed them in water in another frying pan. Soon both meat and vegetable were bubbling away on the wood stove, their fragrances permeating the entire house.

Polly did have a way with her, I had to admit. Later that evening she stirred a bit of thickening into the chicken broth, turning it to a delicious golden gravy.

When Ned stumbled in chilled and soaked from laboring in the heavy snow, one quick whiff sent him charging for the little wood stove.

"You're coping very well," he observed.

"Who, me? Well . . . not really . . ." my voice trailed.

It's a little hard to explain, but Ned didn't seem so aware of Polly's presence as I. He was totally consumed with trying to dig us out, counting the holes in the roof of the house and trailer, figuring out what insurance might pay, etc. And since I somewhat resented Polly's disdain for my valued conveniences, I didn't mind that she often disappeared to another room or otherwise faded into the background when he was around.

The following morning, I rose to stare out at our loved trees, transformed to pitiful ravaged creatures. Now I felt only a deep and wrenching sorrow.

Tall jagged spikes loomed everywhere, protruding from the standing trunks. Many limbs hung downward, broken loose from the mother trunk then caught in a high crotch on their hurtling way earthward. It was as if the trees had tried to grab and rescue some of their precious appendages. Now they hung suspended like swinging gallows victims while they slowly died.

Overcome with despair, I burst into tears. Polly stepped up. "Waste of energy," she said, matter-of-factly. "This house looks almost as much a shambles as the outdoors."

"What can I do?" I sniffled.

"Plenty," Polly admonished with a wide sweep of her arm, "Look around you - wood bark strung about the hearth, reading material everywhere . . ."

My chokecherry jelly and crabapple butter on the kitchen counter caught her attention.

"Admirable accomplishments," she pronounced. I saw a tear light her eye as she gazed past them to the little crabapple tree crouching out in the yard, carried to the ground by its own rosy fruit and the weight of snow.

She snapped back. "Your canning clutters. Depressing. Your man already has plenty to deal with - barley sogging in the windrows, holes in the roof, storage shed split asunder, and yard stacked with trees to be hauled out. What can you do, indeed!"

Pioneer women do have a way of getting down to reality, I thought. We tore into the housework, strained snow water and stored it in jugs in the laundry.

"If we don't need it now," Polly decided, "Houseplants will enjoy it later."

I fetched a box from the miraculously still standing garage to dry wet stovewood. With my canned goods stored away the house looked pleasant, warm and welcoming. My spirits lifted.

But the silent refrigerator and freezer became a gnawing concern. They'd been off more than a day now.

"Unreliable contraptions," Polly grumbled. "Let's carry the food out and pack it in snow drifts. Lord knows, they're plentiful! That should preserve it until your precious electrical power returns. Nice to have, I guess. But my, you are dependent on it, aren't you?"

After a couple of days, the short water supply began to worry me. The more I fretted, the more I itched. "I'd sure like a bath . . ."

Polly heard me, of course. She followed me like a shadow.

"Spit bath," she said abruptly.

"Spit bath?"

"Sure," Polly said. "A gallon of snow water heated on the wood stove and dumped into that fancy little marble basin in your bathroom would suffice. We pioneer folk managed with spit baths many a time when water was short and weather cold. Never lost a body - or a mate."

A trace of mischief tugged at the corners of her usually disciplined lips. As the stress of our situation diminished, her manner seemed to grow lighter, less austere. Maybe she wasn't a total throwback to her pious ancestors in the long flannel nightgowns after all.

The fourth day we were resting after lunch when a sparkling brilliance suddenly flooded the ceiling. The blinding glow yanked my head erect. I squinted.

"REA to the rescue!" I shouted, flinging my arms wide as if to capture the magic before it escaped again.

Ned jumped from his nap on the sofa.

Not to be outdone by rural electric, the sun popped out to join the illumination game. In the yard, the little crabapple tree burst into a glow of its own as dozens of tiny goldfinches descended to feed on its sweet rosy fruit in the snow. All seemed so precisely coordinated, I could almost hear some great voice proclaiming this new genesis.

I ran to the kitchen and turned a knob on my electric stove. A tiny red signal winked back at me from the control panel. The refrigerator and freezer began to hum a merry duet. It was like a lavish Christmas arriving early - all these lovely functioning appliances handed me in a flash.

I had a feeling that somewhere in the background Polly was preparing for departure. I was so busy caressing the gleaming enamel surfaces, I really didn't notice when she moved, ghostlike, out the back door.

Feeling totally in command now, I turned to face Ned who'd stepped up behind me, his face a dance of amusement.

"That pioneer woman really was a whiz, wasn't she?" I commented. "Almost a tyrant."

"What pioneer woman?" Ned sobered and peered into my face. "Are you sure you aren't suffering cabin fever?"

"Yes, I'm sure." I laughed. "I mean the character who took charge when I was so scared and desperate. I actually felt possessed by a real pioneer woman. I don't know how I'd have managed without her."

A twinkle lit Ned's eyes. "She did alright, didn't she?"

"Mm-hmm. I was glad she came but I'm glad she's gone," I said. "She didn't seem to have much use for this modern equipment. And to tell you the truth, I was about fed up with her noble routine anyway."

A MOVING SALE

No day in which you learn something is a complete loss.
- David Eddings

"Call it a moving sale," we were advised. "It'll draw more people."

Actually it was a moving sale. Moving in many ways. We'd sold beautiful Pheasant Crest Farm and would be heading to town. In addition, I was moved from deep gratitude to near hysteria, from compassion to contemplated mayhem.

About 7:30 A.M., a neighbor came by to leave a few things she wanted to sell. Two hours later, without so much as a cup of coffee and maybe breakfast, she was still serving as gracious cashier.

Because of high winds the day before, we couldn't put many items out. Now, a half-hour before the advertised sale time, our yard was so full of cars and enthusiasm you'd have thought we were being shivareed.

To begin, I couldn't find enough tables to display all the "stuff" I'd squirreled away through the years. So I laid my yards and yards of unused sewing fabric out on four old chairs. I'd just gotten the materials arranged when a woman stepped up and brightly announced, "I'll take those chairs."

I burst into wild laughter, threw my arms around the woman and exclaimed, "God bless you!" With one sweep of my arm I sent the fabric to a colorful heap on the ground and sold the chairs.

Ned quickly provided a table by placing an old door atop two steel barrels. It worked fine until he sold the barrels out from under my fabric, vases and other household decor.

Among my friend's contributions to the sale was a set of stemmed glasses very similar to mine. "Oh, you have yours priced much lower," she observed. "Mine probably won't sell."

So I marked mine up to match hers.

They bought hers and left mine.

As I hurried across the yard, someone called, "Betty, your phone is ringing." I raced into the house and grabbed the phone.

"I hear you're having a sale," said the unfamiliar voice at the other end. "Can you direct me to your place?"

I launched into my reply in careful detail, making sure I used precise verbal directions instead of waving my arms and pointing like I usually do.

Suddenly, a huge guffaw came over the line and I recognized the now undisguised voice of our neighbor a half-mile down the road. He didn't need a phone to hear me scream, "I'll clobber you!"

Then there were the books. We set out several boxes to give away. I was reluctant to let them go, but the response was worth watching. Children, in training to read and excited about life's learning opportunities, dug through them with enthusiasm. In contrast, one woman announced, almost proudly, it seemed, "I never read."

Finally, a young woman came, alone, gathered a big armful of my favorite books on how to deal with life, and said in a sad little voice, "I really need these. I'm in the midst of a divorce."

At last. A home for my treasures. A place to be needed. I hoped they might help her find new direction.

Toward the end, my neighbor's soft-bodied, frazzle-haired blond doll remained, almost untouched, until the tiny daughter of a Mexican sugar-beet worker came by. It was love at first sight, but her parents shook their heads. The little girl held the doll to her breast and cried.

Ned reached into his pocket, pulled out money to pay for it and handed the doll to the child. She hugged it tightly and ran to the car.

"Are you sure you should you have done that?" I asked Ned. "Her parents may have been trying to teach her something."

"But I don't understand Spanish," he explained with a smile.

And what of my mischievous neighbor? Eventually, I decided to forgive him for the trick he'd played on me. After all, his wife was still cashiering for us. And he did bring a pot of coffee when he came – a redeeming act, though he may not have known she'd just sold his office chair.

I'm still not sure where that leaves him in this event. But almost any way you look at it, this was really a moving sale.

BACK-DOOR COUNTRY

What you see and hear depends a good deal on where you're standing.   *- C.S. Lewis*

After moving to town, I was asked how I view city life versus country. I'm not sure I'm actually in town. If I could straddle the street out front, I'd have one foot in the city and one in the country, a big step for me physically, but an ideal location, geographically.

On our side of the street, we have city facilities. Across the road, homes with acreages accommodate horses, a few head of cattle, and sometimes sheep. It's nice to have country creatures around with someone else responsible for their care.

I can't say I don't miss the mornings and wildlife on Pheasant Crest Farm. I've lived in and out of town all my life, but there was something rare about that place. It seemed a zone of safety, a haven to wild creatures.

Humans felt that way about it as well. House guests could always be found out on the big redwood deck in early morning, a cup of coffee warming their hands in the cool, fresh air while they stared off into a rosy horizon, contemplating, perhaps, nothing more than the sunrise.

Myriads of birds rocked the treetops with song and deer often strolled through the yard or stood on hind legs to sample apples on the trees. Along with deer, came foxes, badgers . . . and skunks.

The moose that inspired me to write this book apparently declared herself Welcome Wagon hostess when we left. The new owners of Pheasant Crest, concerned for their small children, had to escort her off the premises. And a porcupine tried to claim squatter's rights on the deck. That's simply an uncommon place.

Our new home, while distinctly different, has its own charm. I've been calling it "The Corn Field on The Green," a tongue-in-cheek reference to our peculiar environment. My agronomist mate naturally likes to garden,

Deer feed on crab apples in the yard at Pheasant Crest Farm.

Ned Case photo

so we live amid flowers and vegetables. A prolific sweet-corn field adjoins the driving range of the golf course behind us, defying errant balls that sometimes cuff its tender ears.

I've also found golf balls under tomato vines, looking like dimpled anemic tomatoes. Huge vines hover over them as if hoping to nurse the pale little orbs to rosy-cheeked health.

A view of the Wind River Mountains was a prerequisite to my moving to town. I remembered my parents moving in from the country, then driving up the big hill to the west each evening to watch the sun set behind the mountains. I learned from them that a distant view is essential to the health of a country heart.

From tall, trapezoid-shaped windows in our living room, we watch the mountains perform colorful changes with light and shadow, sunset and storm. Draperies close in our world at night, but leave a sky-high space above where I presume only the moon, God and the birds can peek in.

My husband sees mostly positive differences in the move to town. Trees, so far, consist of one big blue spruce in the front yard. No leaves to rake, automatic sprinklers, lawn mowed in half an hour.

Due to the railroad's recent demolition project, Ned has a huge stack of ties for framing our yard. If he attacks this job with his usual fervor, the only thing that can slow it is a dull chain saw.

So far, he's keeping busy, but it must be quite a change for an active, country-hearted man to trade his 80-acre realm for an 85 by 150 foot lot. If he gets restless, I suppose I could remind him this seemingly small piece of Earth he owns is 4,000 miles deep. One could easily grow tired and content just dreaming of the work involved if that were horizontal real estate.

To sum it up, change is what life is about. Yet some things do remain the same. Visitors still come in the back door, just as at Pheasant Crest Farm. Our amiable city inspector explained this to me.

"It doesn't matter where you live," he said. "Wyoming is simply back-door country."

Thanks, Dave. That gives me the best of both worlds.

PART II

THE PEOPLE

A Tough-Tender Spirit -

Wyomingites, no longer a specific frontier type, have grown to a rainbow tapestry of tough yet tender people. These stories introduce a few of all ages I've known who define the Wyoming spirit, each in his or her own way.

Branding day on a modern Wyoming ranch.

Author's photo

CELEBRATE THE COWBOY - OR GIRL

How many times have I talked with people who have ridden the trails I have ridden, yet see nothing? They passed over the land just to get over it, not to live with it and see it, feel it.
                                                    - Louis L'Amour

"Whatever are all these adults doing?" I asked myself. "Dressing up like cowboys, walking with bowed legs and talking old west lingo . . ." Had they gotten their noses in a fermented barley bag?

At the annual Cowboy Poetry Roundup, I listened, laughed and clapped. A lariat of fun pulled me in. Cares fell away. In the lobby, I watched a cowboy poet shove a piece of pie in his mouth, sputter and spit, then mumble sheepishly, "I mixed pecan pie with my chew."

If that wasn't a cowboy poem aborning, I thought, I don't know what is. Next morning, I pulled on my Levis, slapped my dad's old Stetson on my head and wrote a poem about the event while fixing breakfast. Back at the Roundup, I recited my poem. It was a hit. I was roped and tied.

Yes, in a sense we're playing cowboy. But that's only the surface view.

Cowboying is the heritage of all of us in Wyoming, whether it's recorded in our geneology charts or not. Cowboying fathered our beautiful state and we don't intend to let it die. We keep it alive on our license plates, our newspaper masthead, college football team and numerous other ways.

Furthermore, Wyoming still has plenty of working cowboys. And please don't forget cowgirls, though some of them do the job a bit differently now.

Wyoming author Diana Kouris has spent a part of every year "cowgirling" for as long as she can remember, or ever since she was big enough to stay on a horse.

Until recently, forty-six weeks of the year Diana was a writer, mother and the very feminine wife of a local school administrator. The other six weeks she was a working cowgirl in the fall cattle roundup on her family's ranch. She usually missed the Cowboy Poetry Roundup to play the real game while the rest of us lived it in poetry and dreams.

Each year, I'm amazed that my friend returns without serious injury. Moving from life as a "hot house plant" as she describes herself, to a month and a half of 10-hour days in the saddle chasing errant cattle over endless miles of rough terrain should bring on culture shock, at least. With breakfast long before daylight and no more meals until after dark, often chilled to the bone by freezing rains, you'd think she'd be glad to be done.

But no. Diana returns to her regular life relaxed and fulfilled. She may bring back all varieties of bumps, cuts and bruises, but such escapades in a real cowgirl's view only add color to the experience.

Due to the tragic death of her brother and subsequent sale of the ranch, my friend will likely cowgirl with the rest of us now, mostly in writing and memory. Still, we somehow envy her for having been privileged to live the richness of the western experience that most of us can only pretend, whether we do it in costume, writing, reciting, or simply adding a little bow-legged swagger to our walk.

My father, a full-time farmer and sometime cowboy, lived that experience with joy in later years when his rancher friend Herb asked him to help with spring and fall cattle drives.

After his death, Herb continued to care for my father's loved horse, Ladybird. One day he came over to tell us Ladybird had stepped in a hole in the pasture and broken a leg. Herb explained that he'd had to shoot her, then sadly handed us my father's old saddle. To me, the act spoke a story's poignant ending that begged poetic form. It goes like this:

Resurrection
A weathered old saddle rode home last night,
alone -
in the back of a pickup truck.
Somehow, it seemed he came too . . .
It mounts a crude sawhorse
out in the garage - no match
for his fleet Ladybird,
lost to a sinking pasture hole,
and a hopeless broken limb.
Saddle shoulders, now aging, bulge sinewy hard,
like those of a stubborn old man, hanging on.
The smell of worn leather and sweat pull me close -
I hug that mute, arched piece of crisp hide
to my breast. And tears bathe to life -
a grin, a shout, and a lusty tale,
of cattle drives, wild galloping winds,
and a free-spirit Wyoming cowboy.

Yes, the legend and life still lives. For some, it's everyday reality. For others, it survives in memory and stories or poetry. Either way, those who ride the trail of the cowboy live it, see it and feel it as did the famous western author, Louis L'Amour himself.

WYOMING WOMAN

Civilization no longer needs to open up wilderness; it needs wilderness to open up the still largely unexplored human mind.
- David Rains Wallace

"Wyoming Woman." These words on the new shirt I bought in Jackson Hole introduce me. Does this label require action? Bestow power? Limit or expand my potential?

In the high hills, I feel like a Wyoming mountain woman. True, up here I live in a trailer and rely on a Wyoming man who bounds about in this altitude like a mountain sheep to get my convenience to Brooks Lake. And true, I have batteries to power the lights and propane to fuel the cooking range, refrigerator and furnace.

But outside my trailer I hike the green hills, alert to bear tracks and scat, inhale the crisp fragrance of pines, and thrill to the coyotes' nighttime howls. I savor the trout caught fresh from clear streams at the base of sky high pinnacles, and watch for elk and moose and deer. My heart leaps at the sight of a bluebird, his tiny prism-like feathers translating light from the heavens to a gift of blue for my eyes.

To a true country-loving woman or man, nothing can fill the heart or renew the soul like a few days close to nature, with or without a trailer. Not everyone understands this, however.

At a chuckwagon dinner at the Bar-J Ranch near Jackson, we visit with a couple who complain about what isn't in Yellowstone Park, how scary it is across much of this country because of the sparse population, lack of heavy traffic, and "nothing for the kids to do." I almost choke on my beans.

The disappointed family leaves without waiting for the Bar-J Wranglers' great show of music, banter and all round fun that thousands from across the world come to see and hear time after time. Sadly, our new friends didn't take much of Wyoming with them.

I wonder if they'd appreciate the huge bull moose and his mate munching grass at the Brooks Lake roadside if they saw them. In shiny dark coats, the bull swaying his great velveted antlers from side to side as he eats, I think these animals are a couple of the most handsome creatures I've ever seen. Then I realize - I see through the eyes of a Wyoming woman.

Would those visitors understand why I climb till my knees throb with pain, up steep bear-country hills, to experience the quiet majesty and soft green mists of Jade Lake nestled in the pines? Why I find sheer ecstasy in snuggling into a grassy curve of rocks with my love of many years in this wild dimple of land halfway up the sky-scraping breccia cliffs? Surely, mine is the heart of a Wyoming woman.

And could a skeptic hear music in the monotone hoot of the great horned owl as he sweeps down into the trees on a crisp autumn night? In the call of the mourning dove perched on a telephone line in the lowlands? In the yip-yip-yip of a coyote pack in the distant hills? I know. I hear with the ears of a Wyoming woman.

Things we find exciting in this state are largely nature-made. Yet there's great irony here. Man, the paradox of God's creation, works endlessly at attempting to improve on the natural world, then when he has overdosed on his own inventions, he hurries back to nature for relief and renewal. Does he know his peace when he finds it?

There is healing in these hills. It's in the simple wonders. Like a porcupine waddling across the road late at night as if the trail were all his; in an odd little dipper bird at streams' edge bouncing about as if she has springs in her legs; a wolf or coyote attacking a snowbank to lure a curious mouse to the surface, and in the fresh little pine and aspen trees springing up from seared earth in Yellowstone Park after the forest burns. But one must remain open, invite the experience, or miss the whole reason for coming here.

It is my wish that all visitors, and residents too, might know the way this country speaks to the soul, might see how the shining blue peaks reflect themselves in eyes that seek horizons. They can - if they're receptive to the magic and mystery.

I think I'll wear my new shirt today.

RIDE OF PASSAGE

In the confrontation between the stream and the rocks, the stream always wins - not through strength, but by perseverence.
                                                                — *H. Jackson Brown*

"Once you get organized," the 8-year-old explained to his grandmother, "You'll never want to live any other way."

He'd spent a day putting her small coins in rolls, then decided to make a list of the various denominations for her purse so she'd have ready reference to her wealth. Already a man of foresight and purpose.

At age 12, Matt had us all convinced that he was a single-minded kid. He'd been that way about horses and riding competition for years. When he first rode one of our mares at age 8, I saw her transformed in a flash from the skittish, unpredictable horse I'd felt her to be, to a gentle, disciplined creature. Clearly, she knew the touch of a competent hand.

Matt and his brother Clint are the sons of Rod, now a single father. Ned and I claim them as adopted grandchildren. So while we all admire Matt's horsemanship, it's easy to see why we've hoped he'd bypass the steer riding part of rodeo.

"If you get all crippled up, you'll never be able to enjoy other things in your life," Ned once advised in a firm, grandfatherly way.

Shortly, we were informed Matt had been kicked in the stomach by a rebel horse, had an arm broken and a hand stitched up. He wasn't interested in discussing the injuries. He was too busy displaying the trophies he'd won.

Being that type youngster, you can see why we had no choice but to go to the junior rodeo at Thermopolis to watch him ride steers.

At the indoor arena, I climbed to the top bleacher.

"Will you man the camera, Ned?" Rod asked. "I have to go hold my kid's hand."

I smiled. There seemed some question as to who supported whom around here. I was hugging Matt's quilted vest like a security blanket myself. On the bleachers below, nervous parents discussed kid rodeos, steer riding in particular.

"My son's never going to ride one of those critters while he lives under my roof," declared one father.

A mother added, "I felt sure if mine got hurt the first time that would be the end of it. But he only grew more determined."

Now I was beginning to understand. To the boys, this was a pre-manhood test, a rite of passage.

Soon it was time for the steer riding. We all moved in close for the action. Perched on the fence near the chutes so I wouldn't miss anything, I studied the boys' faces. Jokes and smart cracks were the order of the day. Until they lowered their bodies to the backs of the bawling long-horned steers, that is.

Suddenly, all was dead serious. Some bit a tongue, some chewed a lip. A quiver ran through the tender young arms as they wrapped a gloved hand around the rope, then pressed it into a fist with the other hand. Just before the gate opened, their faces, still soft-skinned and fuzzless, invariably twisted into a grimace that looked to me like a cross between true grit and tears.

But ride they did. Some hung on until the whistle blew, some couldn't. A couple got kicked in the head as they were thrown, but they dusted themselves off and staggered back, white-faced and uncomplaining, to the fence.

Now it was Matt's turn. In one last burst of bravado, he looked toward his dad and grinned.

"Piece o' cake!" he called. Then he climbed into the chute and eased himself to the back of the steer, big and black, red eyes glaring from between its long horns.

Ned climbed onto a barrel and aimed the camera.

I clutched Matt's vest tighter, recalling a University rodeo at Laramie, where we'd watched in horror as a bull did a somersault on a young student's chest.

Matt's ride was over in the time it took the photographer to click the camera five times. And no, he wasn't thrown. He'd ridden the steer beyond the whistle's shriek and placed in the judging. To our amazement, he was still in one piece.

"Did you spur him?" I asked, feigning nonchalance as I handed him the vest I'd been clasping for dear life.

"Can't remember," Matt clipped, sounding more like a man now than a boy. "Let's go eat."

PIUS MOSS, MASTER WEAVER

America is a tune. It must be sung together.
                                        - Gerald Stanley Lee

I once wrote a piece about lineage, making fun of my own even as I wondered why my attitude seemed so cavalier. When Central Wyoming College in Riverton, Wyoming awarded its prestigious Medallion of Honor in 1991 to Pius Moss, an outstanding Arapaho Indian leader and educator, people of several cultures came to learn at his knee. A modest man who obviously lives to give, he taught us in many ways. I learned the strengths of lineage and of cultures interwoven.

Mr. Moss was born in 1915 at Arapaho, Wyoming. He entered St. Stephen's Indian Mission at age five when his mother died. There he was schooled during the time of the Daws Act that directed Native Americans be taught farming and ranching. The act attempted in the process to eliminate tribal cultural traditions. While much of the Arapaho language was wiped out, Pius Moss stubbornly held it in his heart and memory. Later, he worked for many years teaching the language, culture and history he treasured to the students of St. Stephen's school.

Today, the warmth, wit and wisdom of Pius Moss, while strongly oriented toward his Arapaho Indian culture, leaves an imprint on all whose lives he touches, no matter what their background. In his stories and lessons he speaks not only to Indian people, but clearly to humanity itself. True educator that he is, Mr. Moss sees the value of retaining his own heritage and patterns while weaving them into modern life as well.

"Your bow and arrow today," he advises students, "is education. Your buffalo is a job."

Since Mr. Moss was being recognized for outstanding work in the Arapaho Indian culture, the program was expanded to a multi-cultural panel, consisting of Mr.

Central Wyoming College photo

The Central Wyoming College
Medallion of Honor
presented to
Pius Moss
February 4-5, 1991

Moss and others of Indian, Mexican, Oriental, Portuguese and mixed heritage. All conveyed a sensitivity to their ethnic backgrounds that I'd never known. While deeply touched, I found myself almost envious. I wished the panel and time schedule might have included an even greater variety of cultures.

I was impressed by those who treasure their heritage while recognizing a broader sense of this land

and its people as parts of a whole. Since our Maker didn't create any two of us alike in either looks or manner, He must seek variety. That suggests to me that our diversities are to be treasured; yet combined they can benefit all.

Between programs, I thought of my own complicated heritage. I was raised among a mixture of Indian and Caucasian people on the Rosebud Reservation lands of the Lakota Sioux, but German, Dutch and Scotch-Irish blood runs in my veins. My mate is mainly Irish and British. I thought of loved relatives on both sides who share combined Indian and Caucasian blood. What a "duke's mixture" we are. Our ancestors probably didn't know which part to celebrate.

I do remember my grandmother sending pfeffernuesse cookies at Christmas when I was small. Fragrant with spices and citron, I could see they triggered special memories in my mother when they arrived in the mail. But I don't recall she ever made them herself.

The German language she learned in college. She never spoke it at home. Poring over her textbooks as a child, I fancied I might find a key to unlock the entire language for me. (Pius Moss could have told me what a dream that was.)

With the teachings of Pius Moss, and interpretations of cultural heritage by Dr. Joanne McFarland, President of Central Wyoming College, I finally found my niche. Dr. McFarland's words went something like this:

"America, rather than being the giant melting pot it is often called, seems more like a tapestry to me, woven of colorful threads that all fit together to make one beautiful piece of work."

I'm more comfortable now. I may not have close ties to a particular culture, but I'd rather be part of a rainbow tapestry than a bubble in a boiling cauldron.

To commemorate the award of the Medallion of Honor to Pius Moss, additions were made to the Native American collection of books in the college library, a fitting acknowledgement of the teachings of a special human being to his culture and extended community.

Last, but far from least, I note the mark of a truly great man. The warmth and caring that Pius Moss practices toward humanity clearly begins at home. The tenderness with which he speaks of family touched me deeply.

"I've been married 56 years," the 77-year-old told us. "My wife is beautiful. I'd like to be married 56 years more."

My husband told Mr. Moss he hoped he'd make it, and I promised him another Medallion of Honor if he did. Pius Moss pressed our hands in his and threw back his head in laughter, seemingly unaware of the outstanding contribution he'd made to Wyoming's rainbow tapestry, not only that day, but for all time.

* * * * * * * *

Pius Moss died on November 1, 1998. "HENEEYEINO-HUSEENEE," Mr. Moss. You said that's Arapaho for "I am glad you came." We're glad you came. We're eternally enriched.

WHY WAS I NAMED AFTER DEAD PEOPLE?

There is always one moment in childhood when the door opens and lets the future in.   - Graham Greene

"Why was I named after two dead people?" asked 8-year-old Clinton John, visiting from Casper. He stood close beside me at the cookstove.

I gulped. The spoon in the soup kettle I was stirring began to wobble.

It's normal for this inquisitive youngster to bubble questions all day long. But this wasn't your average kid question. Besides, this was the boy who, when his older brother got caught in a sliding van door two years earlier, came to the house with the solemn advice, "Never kiss a hurtin' man!"

He keeps us all alert.

"Why was I named after two dead people?" Clint persisted.

If he'd been adult, I'd have laughed and quipped something like, "Because you weren't named before them." But this youngster was serious and the look in his eyes made it clear he wasn't going to settle for no answer at all, or even a flimsy one.

My brain felt scrambled. How would his parents want me to explain it? Should I even try? What if that vivid imagination created a different picture than I thought I'd painted? Could his little psyche be maimed for life?

An old Chinese proverb flitted through my mind. "The beginning of wisdom is to learn to call things by their right names."

This child was obviously doubtful he'd ever been called by the right names, particularly when their former owners were deceased. And as for wisdom, what little I thought I possessed had just evaporated.

"As I see it, Confucious," I mused, talking back to the proverb, "Beginning of wisdom here is to learn how to answer the question."

"What did you say?" asked the boy.

"I said, let me think on it a minute."

Clint went into the den to watch television, but the "Big Chicken" show was over (except for the one in my kitchen) and women's exercise classes left him cold. I heard footsteps and there he was by my side again at the cookstove.

"I know how they both died," he continued in an ominous tone. "They weren't very old. Why was I named after two dead people?"

By now, I had my own question. Where, when I needed them, were the parents who'd pinned those names on this contemplative kid?

Stalling for time, I dusted the soup liberally with pepper and fell into a fit of sneezing.

"I have to get a tissue," I said and escaped to the bathroom.

When I returned, there he stood, his brown eyes grave and probing.

"*Why*, Betty?"

The muscles in my neck and shoulders began gathering in painful little knots, a sure sign I'd exhausted my evasion tactics. I pushed the tragic plane crash and untimely suicide of his relatives to the back of my mind and launched my explanation with a stutter.

"Well . . . Well . . . I'm sure your parents loved both your uncles very much. So when a wonderful little boy came along that they loved a lot too, it probably seemed a good idea to keep the names alive by giving them to you."

"Just because they loved me so much?"

"I think so," I said.

Clint broke into a smile and skipped off to play, the worried look gone from his eyes. He'd found the only answer he needed. He was loved and wanted, and he wasn't expected to leave this life early as his namesakes had.

Weak-kneed, I stumbled to the medicine cabinet to see if I might find some sort of stress reduction pill tucked in behind the aspirin. And to thank my Maker for a few right words.

THE RUBY HUNTER

Treat a person as he is, and he will remain as he is. Treat him as he could be, and he will become what he should be.

- Jimmy Johnson

Do you know a ruby hunter? I was raised by one on a South Dakota farm we called the "Runs Close" place. My father leased the Rosebud Reservation land from a Lakota Sioux named "Willie Runs Close to The Village," which Willie certainly didn't. Not on that place, anyway.

Patches of soft, sparkling sand lay scattered about the farm, our favorite being in the little ditch between our small sod-banked house and the road.

As children, Mother often sent my two sisters and me to hunt for rubies in the little ditch. I sometimes wondered if she dreamed up the activity to get us out of the house so she could get some work done. Much later, I would come to see her motives in a quite different light.

My sisters and I found the adventure exciting. We spent many happy hours hunting rubies, while the sun warmed our backs and highlighted the tiny red rocks as we patiently flicked through the sand.

We never knew what the little stones really were, but our mother called them rubies and we believed it so. We always expected the next one we uncovered to be a fabulous deep red beauty. But we treasured the small ones too, since she'd reminded us that any stone would become much smaller if cut and polished.

Today, many years later, after mentally panning and assaying the gleanings of this childhood mining venture, I'm beginning to realize my mother's real motivation. It comes after a long and serious look at her time on Earth.

For ruby hunters, life seems infinitely more pleasant than for those who see only dirt in the sand around them. Not that ruby hunters don't have to deal with just as many problems. The one in my life didn't have anything easy.

The daughter of a newspaper publisher, after college and several years of teaching in a country school, she followed her World War I veteran to a long life on the farm. In the Wyoming she loved for 45 years, she raised eight children of her own and her husband's niece. That job finished, she went back to college to update credentials and teach school for six more years before retiring.

At age 80, an auto accident nearly claimed her life.

"She isn't likely to survive," we were told. "If she does, she'll never walk again."

Three years and three surgeries later she was back on her feet to announce with a twinkle in her eye, "If I keep improving at this rate, I'll be in perfect health by the time I die."

Six years after the accident, she lost her loved husband to tragedy.

She's gone on now, too, but looking back to those days on the Runs Close place and the many years that followed, I've come to see she was not only chief mining engineer, but a true ruby hunter herself. She always looked for the best and brightest and loveliest facets of life and of people, the rubies, the valuable gems. Consequently, she found them despite the adversities life dealt her.

Some of her rubies were large ones, some small, but all were keepers to her, whether relatives, friends or simply acquaintances. None needed reshaping or polishing. All were beautiful in their natural state.

I now understand why she sent us to hunt for rubies on the Runs Close place. She hoped we too might recognize the value of ruby hunting, the kind she'd been quietly teaching all along, by her own example.

It's a special privilege to have known a ruby hunter; an even greater one to have had her for a mother. Without ruby hunters, we might all get lost in the sand.

THE WISDOM AND LOGIC OF A THREE-YEAR-OLD

We worry about what a child will be tomorrow, yet we forget that he is someone today.   *- Stacia Tauscher*

It's been a long time since I saw age three. It's also been a long time since I wondered about the thought processes of that age. So when three-year-old Todd came to visit, he immediately noted my need for education.

Todd and I sat at the breakfast counter drinking milk and discussing relationships. Staring into the distance in deep thought, he asked a challenging question. "Is that your grandpa out there with my daddy?"

My brain spun. My grandpa? Surely he could see I looked about Ned's age. I knew I should have crammed for this test.

I let my mind drift backward. I couldn't just leap into three-year-old logic in a matter of seconds. The big, dark-lashed blue eyes beside me stared straight ahead and waited.

Finally, I tuned into a more youthful thought channel and gave an answer I hoped might earn a passing grade.

"I guess he must be my grandpa. He lives with me, doesn't he?"

"Then where's his grandma?" Todd countered.

This time I was a little quicker. "Why that must be me!" I exclaimed, patting my head. "See? We both have some gray hair."

Todd turned to me and the serious look dissolved in a smile. I had us in the right slots now - a grandpa and grandma with someone to belong to.

A few minutes later, Todd heard someone enter the back door. He ran to look, then tore through the house calling to me, "Your grandpa's in! Your grandpa's in!"

"That's good," I said.

"Well, why don't you go to him?" he asked, annoyed.

I ran to my grandpa, threw my arms around him and gave him a warm kiss. My grandpa found the enthusiasm startling. He'd only gone on a short errand.

I turned to face my small instructor and won a smile of approval. The lesson was clear. You'd better show a little exuberance when a grandpa enters the room.

Todd's a high energy person and likes to see life around him moving at his pace. I scrambled to find my orange teddy bear that sings a variety of tunes when you squeeze his feet. I figured I might make a few grade points on this one.

Todd was delighted at first, then grew suspicious. "How can he sing when his mouth isn't talking?" he challenged.

It took me a few seconds to respond, but I was learning.

"I think he's just humming," I said. "Like this." I closed my lips and hummed a part of one tune. He looked pleased.

By now, I was feeling quite proud of my progress in the class of three-year-old enlightenment. But the teddy bear was getting on the nerves of Todd's parents. What he heard as "parade music" for several hours was becoming a pain in the ear to the adults.

"How about putting the bear in that overstuffed chair to rest?" his mom suggested hopefully.

Todd tried it. The adults noted that it did indeed muffle the sound a bit. But not without Todd noticing that it diminished his music.

His dad suggested he also throw a blanket over the singing teddy bear. That was the last straw.

Todd snatched the bear from the chair and announced, "Four minutes 'till parade time!"

But, as with many of life's anticipated events, the parade never came to pass. Not because the bear's batteries ran down as the adults had hoped they might, but because Todd's imagination did.

Almost, that is. He stuffed the singing teddy bear and a couple of others into a handled basket, hung it over his arm, and marched purposefully across the room.

"Going to work," he declared.

Enlightened now by three-year-old wisdom and logic, I understood his action instantly.

Have you ever considered how smoothly the world might run if more people carried a basketful of teddy bears to work instead of a briefcase full of problems?

ROCKS-IN-THE-ROAD MAN

If it weren't for the rocks in its bed, the stream would have no song.   *- Carl Perkins*

While I envision my mother as a ruby hunter, I see my father quite clearly as a "rocks-in-the-road" type of man.

That makes him sound hard, and hard he was not. But by his own admission, if life didn't hand him a challenge, he created one. He needed a rock, so to speak, to move, climb over or disintegrate.

Some of his self-imposed challenges brought pain, to him and to others as well. I tried to respond with compassion. Surely, I thought, his pain must be deeper than mine. To me, compassion might heal, where grudges could only destroy.

Time was when the rocks seemed more like soft, warm sand, before life rolled so many of the big ones his way.

I remember being tossed in the air when I was small, so I could know how it felt to fly. He told me I lived on a pink cloud, so perhaps he thought I should know the physical experience, if only for a moment. When I came down, I was caught in strong, caring arms. He warned me that might not always be so.

I remember being rocked in my grandmother's old oak rocker, with a cherub face carved in the back and flowing hair that extends to the sides. That bit of art has always lent the chair a special aura, since I never knew my father's mother. The chair sits in our bedroom today, revered and treasured.

When my father rocked his eight children in that chair, creative stories poured forth. I suspect he meant to entertain himself and us at the same time.

Often the tales went on and on. One was about a bird picking one kernel of wheat at a time from the granary and carrying it to her chick in a faraway nest. You can imagine how long it took to empty the granary. Probably about the length of time required to put the child in his lap to sleep while he renewed his creative juices.

The man was stubbornly honest. When I wrote a poem about him one Father's Day, he appeared to think it passed muster until he came to the line that read, "He taught us good from bad."

The facial expression that always looked like a smile suddenly changed. "That should be, 'He taught us good *and* bad,'" he muttered.

Maybe so. In my teens I decided I was mature and independent enough to boldly ask, "How would you like to see me behave as you do?" I thought he'd had a drink that day and it seemed a good time to challenge him.

"You do as I say, not as I do!" he roared.

I hadn't counted on his sobering so quickly.

In high school, I once brought home a report card with a "C" on it. He studied it a while and said, "That's only average. You can do better. You're not average."

That may sound like a father who just couldn't believe his kid was like everyone else's. But I never forgot his words. I'd been challenged to become better than I was. What's more, I'd been told I had the tools. My dad believed it so.

In young adulthood, I complained that I felt my mother-in-law bossed me too much.

"She's a good woman," my father said gently. "You could listen and perhaps learn something valuable." Then he paused and grinned. "But always remember you can go home and do as you please."

I've applied this wonderful advice to many situations through the years and shared it with countless others.

Our mother, my father taught us, was right at the top where respect was concerned. She was his love and inspiration, and he taught us to know her as the fountain of ours.

When in later years she was tragically injured in a car accident, my father's big calloused hands claimed an unfamiliar job. He stubbornly became cook, tender nurse and caregiver to his "Chickadee," as he called her.

Now age 80, he drew uncommon strength to move greater boulders than ever before. He was her one-day-at-a-time teacher and inspiration to walk again. To win this battle, he determined, there was no better sword than laughter. Soon the entire situation became a game, an entertaining challenge that brought new strengths to them both.

At age 84, when my mother could walk again, my father died. The Rocks-in-The-Road man had given his last ounce of strength to heal his treasured Ruby-in-The-Sand.

A man less accustomed to rocks might have failed.

DANNY'S VIEW

Look at everything as though you were seeing it either for the first or last time. Then your time on earth will be filled with glory.
- Betty Smith

In a restaurant I watched a little boy somewhere between two and three years old, totally absorbed with a fly, just an old everyday fly buzzing about the room. While adults worried about it landing on their food, the child marveled at the creature's zooming movement.

"There it goes!" he shouted, arms waving and brown eyes adance.

Then, "It's over there!" The chubby fingers shot toward the far side of the room.

Between bursts of enthusiasm, his mother pushed bits of sandwich into his mouth, to him a matter of small concern.

"It's in our window!" the little boy called excitedly to me at the next table. His sunlit blond hair bounced as he squirmed this way and that to track the awesome thing.

I didn't know the family, but the child so caught my attention and curiosity that I stopped by their table on leaving.

"Hi," I said to the little boy. "I noticed you watching that fly. What's your name?"

"Danny," said his mother, "What do you say to the lady?"

"Hi, gorgeous." The small mouth widened in a grin.

Clearly this young man's view of the world was different from mine.

"I think I'll go fix my hair," I mumbled.

Driving home, I considered Danny's view. How could a common fly be that exciting? Yet things do look different through the eyes of children. Apparently everything in this life is wondrous and fascinating to them. I know they're closer to creation than we, but shouldn't the wonder be seen by us all?

If I could attune myself to a child's response to life, I thought, I'd become ever so wise and aware. And if I truly lived each day as if it were my last, wouldn't I savor each thing, big or small, that tugs at my senses?

Now I remembered Linda, a beautiful young woman I'd met several years ago in the Denver Museum of Art. Linda had dark, luxuriant hair, long lashes and tiny smile crinkles around her eyes and rosy mouth. Veins raised along the backs of her hands. Her nails showed healthy little half-moons at the base. Fine hairs filled the pores in her arms and legs.

Trancelike, I stared. Linda didn't move. Suddenly, a huge aching lump filled my throat. She seemed so alive. She wasn't. She never would be. I squeezed my eyelids tight but the tears pushed through.

"So near," I murmured to myself. "Yet so far. . . . ."

Linda lay on a cold marble slab looking exactly like any other human being. Except. Except for that soft waft of air known as breath; that warm divine stir known as life. Her uniquely talented sculptor-creator could not instill that one precious thing.

I'll always remember my visits with Linda and Danny. Linda reminded me of the miracle of life. And Danny taught me to respond to it. I think now I'll look with more reverence on this world - on the fly and the flower, and the awe that shines in the eyes of a child.

WYOMING MAN

We love because it's the only true adventure.

- Nikki Giovanni

Whenever I hear people talking about marriage problems, I want to ask them if they remember why it seemed such a great idea to marry that particular person in the first place. I don't ask, of course, but maybe it's a question worthy of consideration anytime.

Since my mate and I have shared our lives for many years, I decided to query myself. Right off, I remembered he was one of the best dancers at the old Herder's Hall where the Blue Blazers, Bill's Footwarmers and the Guy Davis Band belted out Beer Barrel Polka and San Antonio Rose.

"Good heavens," I can hear my mother exclaim in dismay, "That's a marriage qualification?"

Well, sort of. Natural coordination and grace are valued things. I wasn't particularly blessed with them and nature strives for balance. Score one.

When I barely knew him, a teacher instructed the girls at a high school party to throw their shoes in a heap where the boys would scramble for them to determine refreshment time partners. I was thrilled at how fast he dug my shoe from the pile. Quick and energetic. Good traits.

He let me do a book report for him once. I presume that was because he thought I could do a better job. Intelligent.

And he was a bit bashful. Probably didn't tell other girls he loved them. Probably.

His persistence in driving across the old bridge that was slowly sinking into the irrigation canal in front of our house was impressive. Though I worried that I was fast becoming geographically undatable, the bridge was replaced only after my sisters and I were married. I suspect it was viewed as a test of courage by the boys as well as my father.

"Watch how the young men treat their mothers," my own advised. "That's likely how you'll be treated."

So I did. The first time I visited his home I watched a wild, laughing, shouting water fight. No, not with his mom. With his grandmother. And sure enough, my mother was right. Just yesterday, I wrestled him for a water gun filled with molasses. A social being. Participates in activities.

By now, if you're thinking all these years of marriage were pure luck, you may not understand the logic in this value system. Here are a few examples of the other side of the story.

He's generous with gifts. And though a music box proved a little embarrassing when it tinkled *Strangers in The Night,* flowers on our son's 30th birthday with a thank-you card quite made up for it.

When I returned from an exhausting stint of caring for an ill parent, I was driven to a lovely rose garden to renew my spirit in a spot of quiet beauty where no thought or feeling of pain could touch me.

In Kansas City, at an annual television taping related to his job at the time, I was introduced to an efficient, business-like woman in a tailored suit who clipped about her work as upwardly mobile women of the day were expected to do. When she heard my name, the facade fell away, her face softened and she was just another sister-woman.

"I've been hoping I'd get to meet the one who deserves those lovely crystal bells he buys at the mall downstairs," she said in a wistful tone.

I doubt I deserved them. I don't know what made me eligible. And after conducting an offbeat character study about a fine manly man, I may even concede there was some luck involved in this long marriage.

But if after all these years one can say without coercion, "I'd do it all again," maybe my earlier criteria weren't so flimsy after all.

Or maybe the ways of love are meant to remain a mystery. As author Richard Bach wrote, "Real love stories never have endings."

BIG AND DARK AND DRESSED IN BLACK

Be not forgetful to entertain strangers: for thereby some have entertained angels unaware. - *Hebrews 13:2*

"Do angels come big and dark and dressed in black?" the woman sitting in the pew whispered to her husband beside her.

It was a frosty Christmas Eve in the small Wyoming town. The pastor of the little church built by a congregation's own hands had left without notice, troubled and confused. The church looked lonely and cold, its people in shock.

The night before, the woman in the pew had a dream. She saw herself and her husband alone in the church on Christmas Eve. In the dream, they lined the walks with sand candles and flung open the big front doors. The sound of her brother's beautiful taped music burst into the frosty air of the street as the two knelt at the altar.

In the dream a passing car slowed, its occupants poking curious heads out the windows. Hadn't the little church died after all? The people listened. They thought they heard a voice calling, "Come. Come try once more. This is the night Christ was born. Wondrous things can happen."

Soon, more cars stopped. And more. And more, until the little church was filled with warmth and joy.

Next morning, the woman awoke, puzzled and pondering her dream. What did it all mean? She phoned a friend.

"We'll have a Christmas Eve service," said the friend in a confident voice. "One way or another. It will happen."

Christmas Eve arrived. The woman and her husband drove to the little church in the small town in Wyoming. To their amazement, the church was surrounded by cars, much as a loving mother might cradle a babe in her arms. Much as the woman had seen in her dream.

The couple hurried inside. The church was packed with people, the air charged with anticipation.

Suddenly, a big dark-haired, smiling man appeared before the congregation.

"Indeed we will have a service!" The deep voice boomed, bouncing off the walls. "Let us sing!" And "Joy to The World" took wings and happy voices carried it to a star-filled sky.

"Do angels come big and dark and dressed in black?" the woman whispered again to her husband beside her. A tear left her eye and rolled slowly down her cheek.

"I think so," her husband answered with a break in his voice. His hand tightened over hers. And their voices burst into song.

Wondrous things had indeed come to pass. The little church, once seeming near death, now pulsed with life. And the warmth of Christmas love filled every corner and crevice.

The big dark man had retired once. Maybe twice. But once again he was needed. So he came. And so did his cheery life partner, lighting candles of her own.

It was 10 years before their "temporary tenure" in the little church ended. During those years, the big dark smiling man opened his arms and heart to the entire community, conducting funeral, wedding and church services for member and non-member alike. Despite serious eye surgery and several other health problems, his vision grew. The church, he said, needed repair. With dollars from his pocket, he led; the people followed. The town, he said was beautiful. It could be more so. With dollars from his pocket and shovel in hand, he helped plant stately spruce trees along their small park.

During those 10 years, his wife played the piano each Sunday, though she'd had surgery on painful, arthritic fingers. Almost daily, she drove the 25 miles from her home to work on church projects and visit with "my people," as she called them.

In their eighties, the man, big and dark and dressed in black retired for the third time, along with his candle-lighting lady, still shining like a star beside him. And the congregation of the little church in the small town in Wyoming, along with the entire community sang "Joy to The World," convinced they'd entertained angels, unaware.

OTHER MOTHER

I can't change the direction of the wind, but I can adjust my sails to always reach my destination.   - *Jimmy Dean*

How do you see your mother-in-law on Mother's Day? My own mother taught me to love books and language and to watch for "rubies in the sand." My other mother taught me a lot about life and survival. I'm what I am today because of the influence of both.

Since I worked in the out-of-doors until I left home, I had little opportunity to learn much about cooking. Because she taught me her way, I never had to listen to my husband ask, "Why don't you do it like Mom does?" That alone can strengthen a marriage.

One of the first times I observed Mom's way was when her sons brought several kids, including me, to their country home after a dance, middle of the night. Mom got out of bed, wrapped herself in a robe and pulled pans of homemade cinnamon rolls from the warming oven to serve us with milk. I was almost ready to move in before I'd been asked.

When I was asked, she offered a 10-gallon can (or maybe two) of hard earned cream to help her son buy my engagement ring. I wonder how many things she needed herself.

This tall, slender, half-Irish lady with dancing brown eyes didn't let many things interfere with her work. We both had some adapting to do in that realm, since I saw various parts of living as equally important. I'm not sure she had a choice.

When we disagreed on something, we listened willingly and openly to the other's view. We learned and grew together. Our differences became our teacher.

Always quick to act in an emergency, Mom saved many lives, including that of our small son. When he choked on a candy ironically called a "Life Saver," she upended him and struck him between the shoulders.

Nothing happened. My husband pleaded with God, and Mom became His conduit. Shoving her finger between clenched teeth and a fast closing throat, she finally pulled out the candy and the color returned to our child's face. While I held him close and cried, Mom wiped the blood from her raw finger.

In response to our gushing gratitude, Mom said with a wry smile, "I knew I had to succeed. I couldn't handle you two if I failed."

While seriously dedicated to work and family, Mom was fun-loving and ready to laugh at nearly every disaster as soon as she'd recovered from it. This was one of her great strengths and the stories would be told and retold with gales of laughter.

Her four sons teased her unmercifully. She loved every minute of it. I suspect her patience may have been tried a bit, though, when one of them dunked her in the horse watering tank.

To Mom, everyone was a friend or neighbor. When driving, she automatically waved to every car she met. I once asked her why and received this explanation, "I don't want to miss anyone."

Mom lost her only daughter in an auto accident when the daughter was in her early thirties. And I lost a loved sister. Mom pulled me closer and our kinship grew.

In her last days, I flew from another state to bathe, feed and care for her. I always knew it would be that way. She'd given me so much.

Later, when my own mother was critically injured in a car accident and discouraged with the long struggle toward recovery, she said to me one day, "I've been think-ing a lot about Ned's mother and how she saw hope and humor in every situation. I wish I could talk with her now."

I can't think of a better tribute to my other mother.

ELK MOUNTAIN JIMMY

Jimmy strokes his banjo,
teasing at the strings,
sweet-talking any life that gathers here.

Pied-piper of the forest,
leaning light against a tree;
a tweed cap, jaunty, rakish, rides
the hair cascading down his neck
like a glistening waterfall . . .
His nose descends from hooded eyes
that shadow-dance beneath
their dense thatched eaves;
his mouth curves upward -
a fallen splinter of moon
caught on his chin.
Bulging at the heels, worn shoes
follow tapping, turned in toes,
reluctantly.

His music bursts like many-hued balloons
released to woo the treetops,
and I'm ready to dance on the picnic table . . .

But eyes around me forbid.
One should maintain a little decorum
at a senior citizen picnic.

"What's your pleasure, lady ?"
he calls from under the tree.
I look into the merry smile and see,
- though he's all of 82 -
Jimmy's hair is prematurely white;
I think – he already sees me dancing . . .

I found myself without a camera when I met Jimmy on Elk Mountain. He became a picture in words, published in *The Casper Star's* Annual Arts Edition. Later I learned the poem was clipped from that newspaper by Jimmy's wife and read at his funeral.

HIS OWN MAN

We are made to persist. That's how we find out who we are.
                                                    - Tobias Wolff

I'm writing this on Mother's Day, but being a little contrary I'm going to focus on a man. I've known this particular person for a number of years. In fact, I lived with him for what now seems a rather short period. It was a special time, nonetheless.

Born in this state, he arrived tough yet tender, a typical Wyoming man. Interesting, too. We once watched him refuse money to maintain his principles. The principle being that he didn't intend to pick up a handful of pennies he'd thrown to the ground when he was three.

That's when we suspected the announcements we'd purchased before his birth may actually have been ordered by him. They read, "I'm the new boss here!"

Once he educated us to the fact that he could understand normal adult reasoning, however, he grew more patient with us.

I always suspected he was a survivor type. When he overcame a head-first tumble into the stock watering tank and a solitary ride in a car racing toward an irrigation canal, I knew he'd probably handle most of life's challenges.

I wasn't so sure about myself. At this point, my mother was about to demand custody of her grandson.

Despite, or maybe because of, our early learning experiences together, he grew to be a modest, manly young man with a generous heart. At a large high school event when he was 15 or 16 years of age, he introduced his parents as chaperones, then pulled his startled mother to her feet for the first dance. You can imagine where that placed him in Mom's estimation. I wondered what effect the act might have on the other kids' view of him, or of parents in general. He didn't seem concerned. He simply did it his way.

In his relationship with his father, the two appeared as much at ease working in the yard together as they were rowdy and competitive in a water fight. Or in buttering each other's ears instead of corn at the dinner table.

"How can you stand the rough-housing?" a friend once asked. "They could break a lamp!"

"Lamps are replaceable," I answered. "My husband has only one son; my son but one father."

Besides, I wasn't so wimpy as it might seem. I once overheard this young man confide to a friend, "I may get to go with you, if Mom doesn't get to Dad before I do."

Still, this son was always his own man. When his father offered to furnish half the money for his first car if he earned the other half, he thanked his dad and bought a cheaper car. One he could pay for himself, while gifting his mother with crystal stemware at Christmas.

Today, that independence is interestingly inter-woven with an appealing John Kennedy type of humor and a sensitive response to nature. Like most people's kids, his intelligence seems amazingly advanced beyond that of his parents.

There's much more to be said, of course, but I'll end this one-time sharing of the man with a poem I wrote for him. One woman read it and exclaimed, "That's my son you wrote about!"

Perhaps it's every mother's son.

I've thought so many times I'd like...to try it all again...I feel I've grown much wiser now...I think I'd be more patient, talk much less...Just show you how life works and then...remind you that your choices...determine what you get. And yet...I look at you today and see...a thoughtful, generous son...manly, kind and loving...respecting everyone...A tender guardian of earth's gifts...and now it seems so strange...I'd wished to do it over...For what is there about you...I could ever wish to change?

MR. FINNEGAN

Sometimes you have to look reality in the eye and deny it.
- Garrison Keillor

I knew him 30 years or so, but I didn't always know Mr. Finnegan. You see, he used to be - to me - Mr. Smith or Mr. Jones, or just another busy man, consumed by work, reserved, and very gruff.

Then he retired. Now there was time to muse upon each precious day, to mellow and enjoy, and still to grow.

He dubbed me "Mrs. Murphy," and he became to me delightful "Mr. Finnegan." We met each Monday morning at a backyard clothesline, trading new-role greetings while we hung communal laundry, and shared in merry dialogue a rainbow fantasy.

Then he left this Earth, quite suddenly. It might have seemed to others irreverent and strange, had they heard my last farewell, (but understood to him and me)

"I'll see you Monday, Finnegan," I whispered tenderly.

The above was written many years ago on the death of my father-in-law. He would probably have been quite ill-at-ease to have read it, though he seemed to love the game that age's mellowing allowed him to play.

Recalling those days, I still find it hard to believe a man could change that much. For years he'd hardly talk to me. Except for the rare occasion when he was feeling more genial and took the time to tease me a bit.

I used to wonder if he wasn't well. I kept thinking there must be a real person in there somewhere.

Eventually, I learned that his mother died quite young and his father, unable to care for the children alone, had sent several, including him, to foster homes. Now I began to understand. At the age of nine or ten he left that home when he heard his foster parents talk of changing his name, of removing the last vestige of his sense of self.

And so he wandered, a mere child working here and there for his board and room to survive. A protective emotional wall grew up around him. Those to whom he should have felt closest, he kept at a distance. He'd learned very early to shield himself from the vulnerability of love . . . probably the thing he needed most.

Through the years as his daughter-in-law, I watched. To neighbors and friends he seemed a jolly man, casual and full of light-hearted jokes and stories. At home that was rarely the case. At home, he was vulnerable. There the wall rose up, generally keeping him remote and reserved, often grumpy.

One time when we were leaving, I gave him a quick hug. He was very embarrassed and uncomfortable. I didn't know how else to show him I cared.

Later, he would show me how. We could play this little game at the clothesline we shared between our two homes. We would no longer have to be Dad and Daughter-in-law. We could be "Mrs. Murphy" and "Mr. Finnegan." We could laugh and chatter freely and happily inside these new characters. We could talk about almost anything while we hid the faces of our other selves behind the towels and sheets and shirts we hung on the line.

The relationship grew to be rewarding and fun-filled. Mr. Finnegan, articulate and clever, loved books and remembered nearly everything he'd ever read.

As long as we lived there, the fantasy continued. He grew warmer and more relaxed with everyone. But occasionally I'd question the wisdom of all this make-believe and confide in my mother-in-law.

"Maybe I shouldn't be playing this game with him. Do you really think it's all right?"

"Oh, please don't ever end it," she said. "It means so much to him. And don't worry. Did you know his description of you has always been, 'She's a lady?'"

No, I didn't. I'm sure it was meant as a fine tribute. But I rather hope he liked me better as his Irish friend at the clothesline. Because that's where I found Mr. Finnegan, the real father-in-law. . .of. . . Mrs. Murphy!

BEST OF THE LIVING WEST

I like to write and record songs about the early people of the 18-1900s, that period of time when it really took true grit to live. The character and values of our ancestors were earned.

- Babe Humphrey

Lights! Action! The Bar-J Wranglers are all over the stage, the heartbeat of the audience almost audible. Babe Humphrey breaks into a jig. Son Scott teases and laughs while Bryan, his brother, deadpans as straight man. Tim Hodgson, their "only friend," plays the part of a slightly dim joke butt, and Donnie Cook performs poker-faced, beneath a red flag proclaiming him "Mr. Excitement."

All these antics occur while the music and harmony of five gifted Wyoming entertainers pull their audience back to cowboy days of the early 20th century. Babe and Scott grab guitars, Bryan the bass viol, Tim, a champion fiddler from Idaho, his violin, and Donnie, a variety of instruments, from the dobro to the banjo. Their

Bar-J Wranglers, left to right: Tim Hodgson, Scott, Babe and Bryan Humphrey in performance

show can turn guests, from nuns to chairmen of the board, into foot-stomping, hand-clapping participants.

From June through September, the Wranglers are busy with the family-owned Bar-J Chuckwagon in Jackson Hole. In October, they come down from the hills to perform for the annual Cowboy Poetry Roundup in Riverton, an event begun by Dr. Kent Stockton, a local physician.

Babe Humphrey has watched the galloping growth of the Bar-J program for 22 years, yet he still seems awed by it all.

"It's like they just discovered us out here in the cow pasture," says Babe.

In truth, people from across America and numerous foreign countries have discovered the Bar-J Wranglers. And their Chuckwagon is out in a cow pasture where chuckwagons were in the old West. The Wranglers are making it big time.

"We've been blessed," Babe drawls in a rich, warm voice that teases at one's ears. "But I hope we never grow too big to say 'thank you' to the good people who come to visit us wherever we perform. I hope some of the philosophy we live by comes across in our show."

The Wranglers' devotion to faith and family, combined with a professional, fun-filled performance draws crowds like cowhands to a rodeo. To many, the Wranglers are a subtle reminder of what's missing in today's world. In Babe's words, "People seem hungry for down-home values."

This modest man is no greenhorn to the western scene. He has performed with and counts among his friends such cowboy stage greats as Roy Rogers and the Sons of The Pioneers.

A few years ago, the Bar-J Wranglers did a cattle drive special for The Nashville Network in Red Lodge, Montana with Roy Rogers. One year they participated in a tribute to the early Sons of The Pioneers in the Western Music Festival in Tucson, Arizona.

Although the Bar-J Wranglers' audience for just one summer would pack a pretty large cow pasture, Babe remains a genuine throwback to the old West. He still sees the whole process as country simple.

"We just invite folks to supper and do our show," he explains.

This modest view of an evening with the Bar-J Wranglers may be part of the magic of their success. It might also be seen by their guests as the understatement of the West.

In tourist season, about 730 people arrive each night at the huge, barn-like building called the Bar-J Chuckwagon. Surrounded by waving native grasses, it's located between Jackson and Teton Village. The area actually was once the south pasture of the Wilson Hereford Ranch. It's still part of a working ranch today.

Along with the joshing, singing and yodeling, the Bar-J Wranglers portray every man's dream of what a father-son relationship should be. For many in the audience, it's like coming home to the kinship they'd always longed for.

Humphrey is proud that theirs is a family affair. He gives generous credit to his wife, Martha, who works quietly behind the scenes and "lends strength in the tough times." And he chuckles as he recalls early days with the boys.

"In their teen years," says their dad, "Scott and Bryan didn't tie right into this idea of performing cowboy music. It just wasn't part of the 'in' thing."

Finally, they decided to try it.

"They heard the harmony, sang a few songs and signed a couple of autographs. Now you couldn't pry them off stage with a crowbar," Babe says with a grin. "Kinda like their pop, I guess."

There were definite rules to the game, however, says Babe. The boys had to learn to handle all aspects of the family business, from digging ditches to pounding nails to cooking food and serving guests. All this was part of their education at the same time they were honing their music and performing skills.

Then there was this "last but not least rule." They couldn't perform full-time until they'd finished college.

"Strong families make a strong country," says Humphrey. "In my case, doing what I love to do, with my sons singing with me, I do feel extremely blessed."

Babe finds no difficulty in remembering who to thank for all these blessings. At each performance a huge, laughing, cheering audience falls reverently silent as lights dim and the Wranglers move into a song of inspiration.

Often the show includes a spot for Babe's gratitude to lie softly on the crowd as he half sings, half recites a work that speaks an earnest response to his own life: "I'm drinkin' from my saucer; my cup has overflowed."

Humphrey talks of retirement down the line, of turning the Wranglers over to the younger generation, but his joy and faith in the value of his work hold a tight rein.

"The West is not only a tourist thing, but educational as well," he says. "We have an opportunity to show the world the best of the living West, and in the best way. Wyoming lends endless potential to that."

PART III

NATURE

Enchantment in The Ordinary

Nature's wiles are enchanting to the extreme, yet not to be trifled with. Her charm can fill your heart or end your life. The trick is to show respect, then love. These stories share her mystery and magic.

Snow-capped entrance to Flagg Ranch in January.

Author's photo

*In winter, Old Faithful's billowing steam
hangs as if frozen in the still, frigid air.*

Author's photo

YELLOWSTONE WINTER JOURNAL

What would life be if we had no courage to attempt anything?
                                                    - Vincent Van Gogh

On November 22 of the year 2000, the National Park Service declared that snowmobile use would be phased out in Yellowstone and Grand Teton national parks over the next three years. In 1994, we were uniquely privileged to see and feel the nature of the Park in winter. Following is my journal report of what may soon be viewed as a rare experience.

January 18: I'm more than a little apprehensive. Only a week ago I rolled my snowmobile on a steep hillside. I don't feel fully recovered, emotionally, from that daunting experience. Yet today, my husband and I, with about a dozen others from our home town plan to snowmobile a distance of 70 miles from Flagg Ranch through the Park to West Yellowstone, Montana.

With the temperature clinging to zero, I'm wearing so many layers of clothing under my insulated suit I feel like a plump leftover Santa Claus waddling toward my machine.

My mate and I began this winter sport when he came home with two little blue snowmobiles in his horse trailer.

"You did WHAT?" I gasped. "What did they cost?"

His answers were evasive. "We can't spend half our lives in hibernation," and "I got a good deal on them."

That generally explains how we got to this point, entering Yellowstone Park in mid-winter on a Golden Age card. But to me, 35 miles is a lengthy ride on a snowmobile. Now we're looking at twice that distance, one way.

My little blue machine is roaring and ready, our saddlebags and fannypacks stuffed with food, drink and extra clothing. Wearing helmets that make us look like we have bowling balls for heads, no one hears me wail, "I've changed my mind!" They're off. I leap on my snowmobile and squeeze the throttle.

After a few miles, I begin to relax and look about. I lift my helmet visor briefly. It's intended to deflect the cold wind at this speed, but I find I don't want to miss a smell, sound or sight. I pull the fresh, clear air into my lungs. Everywhere frost-coated pines sparkle in the morning sun. Behind us, the Tetons stand handsome and dignified, like naval officers in full dress reviewing the troops of fog that march in and out of trees along the river below.

Higher and higher we glide into the high country woods. The forest is silent and crisp. An awesome beauty and peace touch my soul. I'm overjoyed that I came to experience this day.

Beside the road, signs inform me we cross the Continental Divide three times. The first elevation reads 7933; the second, 8391. The third sign says only, "Continental Divide." Its elevation is hidden beneath deep snow.

I hold tight to the hot grips on my handlebars, grateful for their comforting heat at this altitude.

Lewis Creek and Lewis Lake lie pristine and unmarked, except for a few footprints in the blanketing snow. I hope wild creatures know the safe spots to walk.

We stop occasionally to get a closer look or a snap-shot of wild animals and birds wintering in this inhospitable land. My camera growls in the cold.

We move on through the desolate, uninhabitable Yellowstone Fire graveyards. A lump fills my throat. Tree skeletons stand stripped and gaunt, casting their haunting black shadows of death across the snow.

Along Firehole River where the water is warmer than in most Park streams, a bull and cow elk who failed to migrate down to the Jackson Hole winter feeding grounds, forage at water's edge. They ignore us as we wade hip-deep snow for closer pictures. Their only concern is food.

Swans float gracefully on the Firehole River. Now and then they push long necks into the water for moss and aquatic plants to eat, leaving only white triangle tails, like a fleet of tiny sailboats on the surface. Swans appear to experience little struggle in the winter survival game.

We stop at Old Faithful for lunch, amazed to see at least 1,000 snowmobiles in the parking lot. We stand in line for food.

A number of snowcoaches have brought less hardy adventurers to visit the winter Park. Snowcoaches and snowmobile mounted Rangers are a blessing no one disputes up here.

We're told of a 10-year-old boy whose machine stopped on the trail. His parents, unbelievably and unknowingly went on without him. A snowcoach picked him up and towed his machine into town for a joyful reunion with his parents.

Old Faithful's eruption is quite different now than in summer, nature's contrasts more striking. A dark piney hillside enhances the plume as it shoots into a deep blue sky. The geyser's steam rolls off into great billowing clouds that hang as if frozen in the still, frigid air. The performance is vivid and spectacular.

Further on, we find the Madison River area heavily populated with bison, swans, ducks and a few elk. A rugged old bison bull stands a little apart, a great piece of hide missing from his rump. An encounter with another bull? A hungry coyote or wolf? One can only guess.

Comfort stations and warming huts are strategically located along the way. I'm told warming huts also contain snack dispensers, but I don't get to the huts for warming or snacks.

By the time women wrestle their way through layers of clothing at the comfort station, they're warm enough. And the men are at their snow machines yelling, "Let's go!" I vow to perfect my envisioned "equal opportunity" invention as soon as possible.

When at last we chug into the town of West Yellowstone, Montana, the sun has sunk behind the horizon and night chill creeps through our clothes. We're ready for a warm motel and hot meals.

Non-migrating elk feed on dried grasses by Firehole River in winter Yellowstone.   - Author's photo

Yellowstone Park bison and a silhouette snowmobiler share the frosty winter trail.   - Author's photo

January 19: The temperature stands at 18 degrees below zero this morning. Snow machines roar through the streets of West Yellowstone all day and all night. Signs everywhere warn, "Park at least 10 feet from buildings." A potential avalanche of snow piled high on each roof explains the signs.

Some of our group go out to play in the snow. I relax and shop, glad I'm not traveling today.

January 20: Only 10 degrees below zero. At breakfast we meet a tiny boy less than two years old and round as a snowball in his puffy insulated suit. On this, his first snowmobile trip over from Idaho Falls, his mom says, "He didn't like the helmet at first. But when he realized everyone else in this strange world wore them, he loved it." He resembles an adorable moonchild as his smile disappears into the helmet.

The child's enthusiasm reminds me what a wide diversity of age this sport allows to experience the winter park. Today, we range from his less than two years to mid-seventies. Possibly older.

About 10 A.M., we begin our 70-mile return trip. Although it's the same route and the weather still clear, many things have changed.

Geyser Basin hangs so heavy with mist I can scarcely see the machine in front of me. Pines stand in huddles at the roadside, holding us to a narrow, eerie corridor. Frost from the geysers' steam hangs on their sagging limbs like rags. They look like Basin bag ladies.

Bison, their coats white with rime, move sluggishly through the fog. The roaring creatures about them are ignored as merely a part of the winter environment. They must conserve their energy. We stop and wait for the bison to pass. They travel off the road. We do not.

We stop at Old Faithful for lunch. Snowmobiles in the parking lot are sparse today. It is Monday.

The miles roll by. Cresting a high hill, I catch a glimpse of the Tetons in the distance, navy blue, white-capped. I'm happy to see them, yet we're still a long way from Flagg Ranch.

When our small city of pickup trucks and trailers finally comes into view, one can almost hear a collective shout of joy above the roar of snow machines. It's been a long trip, but an unequaled experience. Rick, who I'd seen as our leader the whole time, comes to tell us goodbye. "Enjoyed having you along," he says, extending a hand.

"Thanks. I felt safe with a younger person there who knew what we were doing," I respond gratefully.

His eyes widen. "Me? I had no idea what we were doing!"

I'm glad I didn't share my confidence sooner. It might have been more than either of us could handle.

A CRASH COURSE ON SKIING

Did you ever get the feeling that the world was a tuxedo and you were a pair of brown shoes?
- *George Gobel*

A man named Rod, considerably younger than we, decided that Ned and I were still young enough to learn to ski. Who'd teach us? He would, of course. So on a clear, crisp day on Togwotee Pass, Rod began his fantasy.

"Now stand upright and remain stationary while I give you a crash course," he said.

"Crash course?" I croaked. The term had a prophetic ring. Only after he agreed to leave his video camera in the pickup truck did I consent to listen and learn.

First, he showed us how to fasten our bindings. The word "bind" actually means to hamper free movement or natural action. What a vivid description. But bindings are attached only to your toes. This arrangement is apparently considered necessary in the event you grow light-headed at the 11,000 foot altitude and feel moved to try a pirouette on your skis.

Next, you attach yourself to two poles whose length is determined by the distance from the ground to your armpits. But no, you don't get crutches yet. Instead, you place your hands through two strong pieces of leather that tighten as you grasp the poles. Now you're locked in a pillory of skis and poles, ready for public ridicule. And don't fancy the ridicule isn't your due. You'll earn it soon enough.

Rod demonstrated the easiest (he said) way to reverse your course by deftly lifting and turning one ski in the opposite direction. Then, if you can decide where you left the other foot, it's supposed to be a simple maneuver. Deftness wasn't even a part of it. I could just imagine one leg heading north and the other still bent on a southerly route. Or worse yet, both tied in a stevedore's knot.

When instruction was complete, Ned struck out with me close behind. Shortly, he took his first spill. I doubled with laughter. It put me closer to the ground where I was less conspicuous when I went down a second later. Why did you think I stayed behind?

After a time, we gained a modicum of confidence and soon our tense bodies loosened and strides lengthened. Nothing approaching professionalism, but you might say we bordered on short spurts of grace.

Suddenly, I came to an abrupt halt. I flopped forward, then regained my balance. I tried to lift my left ski. It wouldn't move. Must be caught on a weed beneath the snow, I thought. Cautiously, I squatted and brushed the two or three inches of soft powder off my skis.

What a tricky little performance. I'd made a neat X by crossing my skis and now held the left one down with the right. Uncrossing them seemed such a simple thing. It wasn't. After a few minutes of awkward struggle, I didn't know my right foot from my left.

I'll just topple over, I decided, straighten them out and be on my feet in seconds. When I fancied I was ready to whip to an upright position, I discovered my hands were totally unavailable to assist, they being still held in a blackwall hitch by the thong loop on my poles. Pushing myself to my feet with the poles didn't work, either. In this position, their only value is to prevent you from clamping your hands beneath your skis, too.

After a lengthy struggle that must surely have resembled the last throes of some dying critter, I summoned enough coordinating muscles to flounder to my feet. Clearly, Rod hadn't revealed any tactical procedure to cover this exercise.

As my body wearied, my mind came alive with the earlier advice of our son: "Now don't forget Rule No. 1: The distance back to your vehicle is at least equal to the distance you've skied away from it."

I could see the pickup truck from the snowbank where I was again held hostage. Suddenly, I recalled

Rod's last words before he and Ned skied off into the white reaches of Togwotee: "If all else fails, just take 'em the hell off!"

So I did. Feather-footed, I walked back to the pickup, praising Rod for the best advice he'd given me all day.

SKEPTIC IN AN ENCHANTED WORLD

The trail is the thing, not the end of the trail. Travel too fast and you miss all you are traveling for — Louis L'Amour

It's only a year since I greeted my mate with disparaging (some say smart aleck) remarks when he brought two howling snow machines home in his horse trailer. Can a person revert in one 12-month period from sarcastic skeptic to snowmobile nut? I didn't think it could happen.

To begin, I was afraid of the critters. They seemed so contrary; something in the character of a mule. Just try to get one to turn around in less than five yards. Sure, you can lift its rear end and head it in another direction. You can turn a mule around that way, too, if you can lift it.

Furthermore, snowmobiles are distressingly noisy. Did you know the word "noise" is derived from the Latin word "nausea?" Honest! No wonder my early response lacked grace.

Ned has since bought a tilt trailer to haul the machines. And though one of the excitable beasts leaped completely over the trailer in an early loading, they're now quite tame and obedient.

Our first trip carried me much deeper into winter's magic than I could ever have traveled on foot or ski. Still, I rode much like I first rode a horse, tense and filled with trepidation. Consequently, my body and soul were totally out of sync.

Then, just before Christmas, we rode seven miles into the forest on Flagstaff road in the Togwotee Pass area. A heavy new snowfall decorated every tree. No size or shape seemed more qualified than the other to be dubbed "Most Beautiful Christmas Tree."

On a road that bore no tracks, the quiet forest echoed back the roar of our snow machines. My heart filled with awe at nature's magnificent art, and I whispered apologies for assaulting the hallowed silence.

All the way in, we watched for wildlife but saw nothing. On return, we were startled to see the trail we'd just traveled completely filled with tracks. Had the wild animals heard our machines and followed to see what the bellowing creatures might be? They showed us only snowy footprints that day. But clearly they'd followed us in.

On Union Pass at the new year's beginning, a small herd of moose lay in the willows less than a half-mile from where we rode. Our racket seemed not to disturb them at all. We stopped to share a reciprocal staring. Neither we nor they grew alarmed at the presence of the other.

Slowly, I began to feel more friendly toward my transporting equipment. If wildlife had no fear, why should I? The more I relaxed, the more I felt a part of my machine and the less it bucked and shied. We were beginning to move in rhythm. More like a good horse and rider.

On a given wintry morning now, the mountains call to my mate. I look out the window. Snowy and windy up there, I think. Not a good day for snowmobiling. But he is ready and waiting. I layer my reluctant body with clothes and we're off.

At the Tie Hack Monument, he unloads his machine. I cling to the warm pickup as he moves out of sight. Shortly, he returns.

"You really should come," he urges. "It's great out there!"

Together, we stuff me and my many layers of clothing into an insulated suit and take off. Truly, it is gorgeous. We look through a curtain of huge wet flakes as we ride. Across the draw, gusts of wind lift snow from the pines in great swirling clouds, then sift them among red and gold willows lining the creek below.

Up, up we glide into the high country woods, a totally different realm. Here, despite the snow machine's roar, I feel the forest silence wrap around me. A lump comes to my throat and tears to my eyes. Here lives awesome beauty and peace, surely nature's imprint of the divine.

I wonder to myself if this might be the retreat of the Great Spirit. When it tires of the clamor, complaining and pleading for favors below, what a heavenly place to recoup. I'm overjoyed that I came to experience this day.

No, you won't see our vehicles racing over the hills and valleys, ducking frantically in and out among others on the trail. Ours is a search for ambiance, for a fresh view of winter, a new mood and message from nature. Frequently, we stop and quiet our motors to absorb the serenity of the winter woods, sometimes to picnic in the snow.

It's an enchanted world. Our little blue snow machines take us there.

ONE CANDY BAR AND THREE CARTONS OF WORMS

Sometimes the road less traveled is less traveled for a reason
- Jerry Seinfeld

May 16 - Surely, springtime in the Rockies! Stressed by life and concern over water in the lowlands, my mate begins pushing for a mountain fishing trip.

I love the high country. But I no longer consent to "tenting on the old campground" as they did in a World War I song my father sang.

Somewhere in time travel trailers came into being with refrigerator, range and a comfortable bed and bath. I fell victim to ease in the wilderness. It's something a naturalist would abhor, but a man who wants his wife up there fishing with him soon learns to use this bait. We stock the trailer and head for the hills.

In Dubois, we decide to check with the Forest Service on the condition of Brooks Lake Road. They haven't been in there and can provide no current information. "But just in case," says the ranger, "I'd leave that trailer at the highway if I were you. At least until you check out the road."

At Brooks Lake turnoff, everything looks dry and clear as far as we can see. We decide to take the ranger's advice, though. We unhook the trailer and leave it at roadside.

About a mile up Brooks Lake Road, we note small snowbanks here and there. Soon we come upon strange clumps of snow lining the road and borrowpits. They resemble huge tree stumps that take on size and foreboding shapes as we drive.

The road, now entirely snow-covered, has been cleared somewhat with a narrow blade, barely the width of our pickup truck. By now, snowpack in all directions has increased dramatically and turn-around is impossible. We engage the 4-wheel drive and push on.

Shortly, we're surrounded by menacing looking white snow figures that loom over us, taller than the truck cab. Standing tightly grouped on both sides of the road, they grab at our hubcaps and slap the side mirrors back against the truck body. On this once familiar trail, we feel like aliens in a foreign land.

The ghostly guards herd us further down the narrow lane. I find it frightening to be deprived of the choice of turning back. There's no way to know what lies ahead.

Snow continues to pile higher. To stave off panic, I try to make light of our situation. "I guess you know if we get stalled, our survival depends on one candy bar and three cartons of night crawlers."

Ned grimaces. "I choose the candy bar."

I hadn't meant to give him a choice.

In this eerie world, we're confined to a deep white pit with the giant snow ghosts directing us at will. I'm at once humbled and apprehensive of this strange control. Ned is mostly silent, his attention of necessity given to managing our vehicle in the deep icy ruts.

We creep along in 4-wheel drive and finally arrive at Brooks Lake Lodge. There's no road in and no trail to the lake itself. This mid-May, all still lies beneath several feet of ice and snow. Except for the two of us, no sign of human or animal life is evident.

In a small area near the deserted caretaker's cabin just inside the lodge gate, we manage to turn our pickup around by backing two or three feet, advancing a few, backing, then advancing.

At last we're headed out. We move, in a distance of four or five miles, from a world we'd never imagined to a clear dry road with no sign of snow. It's a weird transition. Like Alice in Wonderland emerging from the rabbit hole.

Back at the highway turnoff, our travel trailer fairly glows as it comes into view.

"Wonder who'd leave a precious haven like that sitting along the road?" I venture.

"Probably a couple of very lucky people who took the advice of a forest ranger," Ned replies.

Springtime in the Rockies? Hmm-m-m.

A WAYWARD WIND

The pessimist complains about the wind; the optimist expects it to change; the realist adjusts the sails. - William Arthur Ward

An old proverb says, "It's an ill wind that blows nobody good."

I used to ponder that clumsy sentence as a child, wondering where in the world its wisdom was hidden. I knew it had to be there. How else would it have come to be such a respected and oft-quoted maxim?

One thing I'm sure of, Wyoming wind has blown us real good lately. It has blown the neighbor's old tree branches and a big plastic tarp plus a few boxes and bags at least half a mile to our place. It ripped the protective burlap and wire off some of our junipers one night and Ned hunted for hours to find them. It blew a beautiful horned lark into an REA wire and killed it.

And there's more. In our first year at Pheasant Crest, after a day of leaf burning we meticulously hosed everything down. About midnight, I awoke to hear the wind howling through the treetops and Ned's feet hitting the floor as he jumped into jeans and boots and raced out the door. From the window, I saw pieces of dead branches and debris dancing around our yard, each waving its own glowing torch and igniting new flames as it traveled.

While Ned battled to hose down an area of old manure burning in the corrals, I ran with a bucket full of water to douse a now-flaming log across the irrigation ditch behind the house. I thought I remembered it as a small ditch. I was wrong.

Poised on its bank in the darkened area where the security light doesn't reach, I proceeded to leap lightly across with the bucket. The cat stepped in front of me and I plunged backend over breadbasket into a main lateral several feet deep. I knew exactly how Alice in Wonderland felt when she tumbled down the rabbit hole.

I lay there wondering how many parts of me were broken and if Ned would ever find me in case the situation reached the point where he'd miss me. If the house burned, he'd think I perished in the fire. Meantime, here I'd be, already half-buried in an irrigation ditch, all because of a logy cat and a rogue wind. Truth was, I couldn't have begun to leap that ditch, even if all else had been in my favor.

Eventually, I discovered I could crawl and reached the house where I nursed my darkening leg and stayed put lest I create more havoc. There were no broken bones but the doctor's suggestion of exploratory surgery left me content to wait out the several months of healing.

The best part is, we saved our home. And despite close calls when we perhaps hadn't yet learned a proper respect for Wyoming wind, it does have its good properties. Wind sweeps out smog from our valley, keeping the air fresh and clean. That's a blessing. It removes cold air and sometimes leaves behind a chinook, that magical breath of spring in mid-winter.

So if it seems the wayward wind is a sickie that blows nobody good some days, believe it. There are days like that. Other times, you can balance it off by remembering it would be unusual if someone didn't in some way benefit. Simply adjust it to your mood. Come to think of it, maybe that's why the proverb is written as it is.

A HORIZONTAL DEPTH FINDER?

Smooth seas do not make skillful sailors.   *- African proverb*

"I wish I had a depth finder for my boat," said my mate one morning.

"Aha," I said to myself. "An idea for Father's Day."

The expense of replacing propellers damaged in unexpected shallows had caused him to announce he was going "to sell the damned old thing." I didn't think he really meant it.

We got the depth finder and he installed it. "Let's drive down to Boysen Lake and check it out," he suggested soon after.

At Boysen, we launched the boat and flipped the starter switch. Our motor burst into a happy hum. Several more youthful crafts sat struggling and sputtering as their owners administered first-aid with starter cables and carburetor gas transfusions.

I'd supposed my part in this excursion would be to pack a lunch, then relax in a comfortable upholstered seat under the boat's cool canopy, drinking an ice-cold Pepsi and munching potato chips. Time for a reality check.

Out on the water, I soon discovered I was expected to man (or woman) the helm, a position I don't particularly relish. I'd had my fill of that when I operated the boat for water skiing, too chicken to participate otherwise. In addition, I now found myself in charge of the new depth finder, a gadget of no special interest to me beyond the fact that it pleased my mate.

And whose Father's Day gift was this, anyway?

By now, I suppose you're wondering what the gift recipient himself was doing. I wondered too, until I turned to see him monitoring both our fishing lines trolling along behind the boat while I, hopefully, kept us off the shallow reefs and into schools upon schools of fish. (Large size, please, while you're at it.)

Well, the depth finder has a few delusions about its talents. While it faithfully apprised me of safe depths, it kept teasing me with cute little pictures of computerized fish forms. I quickly relayed the instrument's messages to my shipmate. At the depth of 80 to 90 feet, I announced the appearance of a Loch Boysen monster on my screen. None of this excited anyone but me.

The depth finder truly won its place in my heart when it shot forth the message that we'd moved in seconds from a depth of 80 feet to 16, over an unseen reef. I spun the wheel faster than I ever knew I could move.

When we headed for shore, my fellow seaman grinned and commented happily, "Pretty good ol' boat after all, huh?" The vessel and depth finder had both passed the test. The helmsman, to my dismay, was still on trial.

Just when I expected him to take over, my mate informed me he'd back the trailer down the ramp and I could put the boat into dock and yes, onto its trailer.

I'd never done this before. I never intended to.

With an audience of several men still trying to get their boats started and by now in desperate need of a laugh, I made a couple of unsuccessful tries to get the contrary critter inside two upright poles on the trailer.

On the third try, the one that's known as a charm, I called up all my feminine sense of spatial perception, headed in without throttling down enough and landed squarely between the poles, almost into the back of the pickup truck.

"Uh - you should have come in a little slower," advised my mate, regaining his foothold after a sudden backward leap to safety. Then, realizing he might be in dangerous waters himself, he quickly added, "But you did OK! You did OK!"

If you should ever hear of a horizontal depth finder, could you please give me a call?

PRE-WINTER MOUNTAINS

The winter wind is the fierce breath of change itself. . .
                                                    - Hal Borland

Was that white stuff on our roof in August a late spring frost or an early fall one? Whatever, the frozen water hoses at our Brooks Lake Campground are usually enough to head us downhill to a warm home for the winter.

It's always hard to leave that area, though. The high country emits a magic of its own. A part of that is a haunting awareness that pulls us into its realm and instills a need for more.

Reluctant to yield to winter's early warnings, we climb a high knoll overlooking endless valleys below the narrow dirt mountain road between Brooks and Wind River Lakes. I'm afraid of that road. I doubt we should even be on the knoll with a storm heading our way. But we stay.

While Ned experiments with a video camera, I watch dark clouds roll in. Thunder claps seem to have no end. Behind me loom the sky-high rock pinnacles. I turn and listen, enchanted, as thunder rolls along the craggy cliffs, roaring and echoing until its last growl finds escape at the end of the huge escarpment, literally swallowed by thin air.

As we do each year, we make a last drive through Yellowstone Park to see what has changed since the devastating 1988 forest fires. After the first years, much still looks bleak and dead. In severe hot spots where all life was destroyed and the land made sterile for a time, only clumps of coarse grass grow. Where trees were killed but the ground not seared, new pines spring up, about 12 or 15 inches tall. We neither see nor hear signs of wildlife in any of the burn areas in these early post-fire years. Later, when there's food and cover, they'll likely return.

Driving through many miles of blackened skeleton trees that give up still more of themselves as their bark peels and drops to the ground, one can easily grow depressed. Then we remember that nature is not in such a hurry to repair her injuries as we humans are. We see ourselves basically in a one-lifetime sort of frame here on Earth, whereas nature applies a more patient, relaxed measure of herself.

We drive on toward the east gate of the Park and enjoy a healthier looking forest life. We're well rewarded. On Sylvan Pass, we come upon a big black bear feeding on grass in the ditch beside the road. I roll down the window and begin snapping pictures as he calmly continues to eat. When another car stops, he notes the growing human population, digs his claws into a fallen log and bounds to the top of the steep embankment and into the dense forest.

Back at our trailer, we rise early next morning to hear the Brooks Lake Lodge wrangler call in his horses.

"Yah-ho!" His voice echoes among the pines and bounces back and forth between the great stone cliffs. "Yah-ho!"

Thirty or more saddle horses come running from the lush green hillside where they've grazed overnight. The sun peers over the pinnacles and paints vivid reflections of tree-covered hills in the lake.

Often we stay in the high country until after everyone leaves, even the camp host. A part of winding down our summer is finding ourselves alone up there, waking to heavy-frosted mornings, walking along the lake, frozen grasses crunching loudly under our boots.

Wildlife moves in closer now. In the dark night, we waken each other to whisper, "Listen. Coyotes are howling in the hills." Or, "Hear the owls hooting in the pines?" And sometimes, (me) "Is that a bull moose or a grizzly rubbing against the trailer?"

Finally, lonely for other humans as the pre-winter mountain weather threatens, we hook up our rig and happily descend to a lower altitude where hopefully, winter is a month or two away. If we're lucky.

WHEN NATURE CELEBRATES

Though we travel the world over to find the beautiful, we must carry it with us or we find it not.   *- Ralph Waldo Emerson*

In many parts of the country, a sunset is only a sunset. In Wyoming the entire sky celebrates. When clouds linger here and there like bashful wallflowers at a dance, they are quickly draped in rainbow gowns and drawn into the drama of the skies. At times, even the landscape joins in. Wouldn't it be sad to miss such a show simply because we'd failed to observe?

Emerson said we must carry the beautiful with us or find it not. Was he saying we must carry with us anticipation? An awareness that allows us to be still, to really see and appreciate beauty wherever it is and in whatever form?

One winter evening at Pheasant Crest, as the sun dropped behind the Rockies we watched the heavens in every direction come abloom with a soft rosy glow. Through the dark silhouette boughs of a row of huge willow trees to the north of our yard, golden barley stubbles absorbed and reflected the beautiful blush.

The paired owls in the elms began to hoot back and forth. Our friendly namesake pheasant out by the woodpile sounded a long, loud evening call. Were the birds, like we, simply feeling that glorious sunset was something to shout about?

Ned and I hurried through the house, exclaiming to each other that the scene was most colorful from this window or that. But we were mistaken. The splendor was everywhere.

When the color-deepening horizon stained the ecru lace curtains in the living room a lovely apricot shade, enchantment moved inside. I wondered if I'd have chosen that color had it been available when I purchased the curtains. No, I decided, I prefer the ecru. That way nature can surprise me by tinting them any color compatible with her scheme of the moment.

As dusk moved in to cloak the evening in shadows, we turned from the windows to sit in the warmth of our little wood stove and consider other kaleidoscope hues nature adds to our lives.

When we drive home from Riverton, we turn north on the Eight-Mile Road into an ever-changing view of the Owl Creek Mountains. Sometimes they're in a navy blue mood, dark and brooding, emitting no light at all. More often, they seem to dance in pastels of lavender, blue and rose, with only the deep folds of their skirts concealed in shadow.

Occasionally, I'm positive a mirage has lifted into being a huge promontory that doesn't exist in that spot day to day. But when the landscape appears flat and dull, obscured by phantom clouds, it seems only to lend privacy while the mountains are changing clothes. Often, as the sun descends and clouds lift, the Owl Creeks emerge in soft snowy nightgowns that they quickly fling aside the next day. A peak to the west looms above all wearing a glowing gold and ruby crown of sunlit snow as if to announce its royal guardianship, appointed purely by size.

When we share such natural beauties with a child and heighten his awareness of them, we give an invaluable gift. From the time our son was very small, his father carried him outside in the evenings to marvel at the glory of sunsets. As soon as the child could speak, his chubby arms would wave at the skies nearly every time he went outside and a line of wonder would echo back, "Oh, see pitty sunset!"

Whether the sun was actually setting or not, we were expected to respond with enthusiasm, and did.

To this day, our son lives in awe of nature's drama, gives the stresses of his life and work to the outdoors, feeds his soul on its endless beauty and renewing strengths. Is there a better gift anywhere to carry through life?

Wyoming is particularly generous with such blessings if we but avail ourselves. What's more, they're free.

NATURE MAY HAVE ME SNOWED

When I no longer thrill to the first snow of the season, I'll know
I'm growing old.   *- Lady Bird Johnson*

It seems a bit strange that snow should be a fascination to one who's spent so many years in Wyoming. But we lived more southerly for a time, so now its crystalline magic is new again.

Each fall, when snow covers the ground I feel the same awareness of its sparkling beauty I knew in childhood, seeing all its colors instead of just white. It freshens my senses along with the land.

Hiking to the end of our farm on a winter morning, a curious variety of tracks makes me wonder if the wild creatures have been playing the snow game of fox and goose. I shiver. Maybe it's fox and our protected pheasants. I wonder if they wonder about my tracks.

At the end of the pasture, glistening little balls about an inch in diameter hang like chains of rhinestones on the east fence. In a slight breeze, on a single strand, one ball twirls one direction, the next ball the other. How can that be?

Curious and enchanted, I run my fingers down the chain to discover the beads are frost crystals strung on hairs from the horses' tails. Nature, like the early Indians, uses simple, at-hand products for her remarkable art. But I still don't know how the beads can twirl in opposite directions.

Winter in Wyoming is exciting. Of course, your view may depend on whether you're sailing merrily down a ski slope or hanging in traction after slipping on ice. And three or four days of soupy fog wasn't what I had in mind when I said, "How about a little variety?"

Still, the snow and heavy frost decorating trees and fences made this country a near magical place. And since the fog gave birth to much of the beauty, I won't complain.

A recent evening trip to town was full of surprises. Every time I neared a roadside tree as I drove, I found myself in a sudden shower of snow and frost, an unsuspecting target for the mischievous blasts. Between trees, all was quiet. How could that be? Do trees grab wind gusts like they snatch Charlie Brown's kite in the Peanuts comic strip?

Driving over Togwotee Pass on a warm day in autumn, we watched blobs of slightly thawing snow drop from tree limbs, then roll down a hill rounding themselves as they traveled and grew. Behind, they left ever deepening trails. Finally, the large spheres lay dripping in a draw at the bottom like a colony of fat snowmen exhausted and sweating from their reckless race down the hill.

Sometimes, several balls rolled down the same track, then fanned out on divided trails at the bottom to create a unique design, almost like a shadow of the tree from which they fell.

One January after snow had lain so deep and hay was so scarce that livestock died searching for feed, capricious Wyoming winds suddenly melted the heavy snow to the ground. There, we were delighted to find live alyssum still bearing bright purple blossoms, and daisies, hollyhocks, poppies and flax, all still sporting green foliage. Spring in January, for a time.

Snow creates the unbelievable in both directions in this variable country. Either extreme can be an enchanting experience if you're receptive to wonder. Or gullible. Webster, who due to my schoolteacher mother haunts my every word, reminds me there's a chance nature just has me snowed.

CHRISTMAS CARD SCENE COME ALIVE

I like trees because they seem more resigned to the way they have to live than other things do.   *- Willa Cather*

"Let's go to the mountains for a Christmas tree," calls my mate on a clear crisp morning in December.

"Where?" I ask.

"Sheridan Creek Road."

I fill the thermos with coffee, tuck fried chicken and spice cake into the picnic box, and layer my body with clothes. All the way to Dubois, I scan the high hills. Is there enough snow to accommodate our machines? The forecast of mountain storms every two or three days must surely have missed it this time. Too many brown spots up there.

A few misty clouds creep along the peaks. We can't tell if it's snowing or just rearranging what's already there.

"We'll probably have to drive all the way to Togwotee Pass to unload the snowmobiles," I say. I enjoy the drive, but I get nervous where vehicles charge in every direction, powered by the hot blood of drivers who must prove their snow machine is bigger, louder, or that I'd make a good target for their game of Russian Roulette in the snow.

East of Crowheart, a lone moose grazes a hillside near the road. I wonder why he's so far from the mountains. Then I remember it was a moose at our country home that first inspired me to write about Wyoming's mystery and magic. I recall the bear we saw ambling along the ridge near Dubois one fall, and that one visited our hometown another year. Maybe they wonder why we're in their territory.

Down by the river, a bald eagle surveys the area, his white head and tail shining like beacons from the tall, leafless tree.

At the Sheridan Creek turnoff, we stop to check the trail. It's covered with several inches of snow. So much for my predictions.

We unload the snowmobiles. While Ned ties the little Red Flyer sled behind his machine and loads his axe, I fill saddlebags with food. Our snowmobiles roar and tug at the snow. Slowly we glide up the hills toward Sheridan Pass. In the quiet, thickening forest, we savor the silence, breathe deeply of the fresh pine fragrance. I lift my helmet visor. The crisp cold air tingles my face. Snowflakes begin floating softly through the air.

A blizzard of birds drops from the sky, whips down toward the trail, then shoots upward to disappear over the trees.

Suddenly, on a steep hill the road ahead glares, covered with yards and yards of thick, rough ice.

Apparently a culvert under the road became plugged with debris, then when snow thawed very fast one warm day, water overflowed the road. A sudden cold wave turned it to an ice field.

I'm petrified with fear. If my machine should start sliding to the left, I could roll for miles down the steep sidehill to the canyon below.

"I'm not going to cross this am I?" I croak. I look about. There's no way around the ice.

No way to turn back.

Ned has already crossed the long ice strip. He turns to watch me with a worried look.

"Just don't stop!" he warns. "Stay to the inside and keep going. Otherwise, you'll start to slide."

"Start to slide?" I wail. By now I have both feet on the ground, no, on the ice, trying to keep from heading for the valley. The altitude couldn't have taken my breath any faster than this situation. And if I get safely up the hill, I'll still have to come back, sliding down the incline across very dangerous ice. I've never been closer to utter panic.

Dragging one foot to keep my machine from sliding to the left, I inch on. Finally, I'm across the ice and back on the trail. My snowmobile grabs the snow and hangs on, seemingly as glad for traction as I. I inhale and the icy air swells my lungs . I didn't know I could hold my breath for so long.

We ride higher into the woods. There on a steep hillside stands the loveliest tree in the forest - tall, graceful, and heavy with lush green needles.

"This is it!" Ned struggles through deep snow to its side. I stand on more level land hanging onto a rope tied to the tree so it won't slide down the hill. If I let the tree fall the wrong way, I wonder, could I be catapulted to the next ridge?

Deftly, Ned chops away at the trunk. The tree shudders, then topples into a snowbank.

For a second, I drop my head and squeeze my eyes tight. Each time I see a tree severed from Earth, a strange sorrow fills my heart. What does this mean? Are we some sort of mysterious kin?

I don't know what to do with the feeling and put it behind me. We tie the tree to the sled to transport it back to the pickup truck. The little Red Flyer creaks under the big tree.

Driving down from the high hills, we see the mysterious "frostbows" we've experienced before, following us through the mountains as we drive. They're similar to rainbows, except that the air is filled with frost instead of mist. It's a hauntingly beautiful sight.

In our living room next day, the tree stands dressed in colorful decorations, handmade, boughten, gifted, and treasured.

"It should have descended the hills in a golden chariot!" I exclaim.

Ned's down-to-earth view puts the scene in touching perspective.

"It's Christmas," he says in a soft voice. "Maybe a child's little Red Flyer was more appropriate."

SLOW MOVING WINTER

There is nothing worse than a sharp image of a fuzzy concept.
- Ansel Adams

Wyoming winters often see trees and chainlink fences for a time in February draped in crystalline magic. Fog becomes dense and even window screens and cobwebs under the eaves hang heavy with frost. I've often greeted people with, "Isn't it awesome?"

At first they agree. But after perhaps two weeks of fog and hoar frost, some have been known to ask, "Don't you recognize an overdose of awe when you see it?"

Now the response to my greeting becomes, "It's making me depressed."

A television documentary on Finland, where the population is said to be perpetually melancholy, has grown to be a popular topic of conversation. At their dances, couples embrace and whirl about kicking up their heels. Looks like great fun. Yet not one dancer wears a hint of a smile.

I've read this is a natural reaction to a shortage of sunshine. Lest we become as glum as our Finnish friends, I'm offering several ways to deal with a slow-moving winter.

1. Talk to God. After church one gray Sunday, a friend confided, "I prayed God would send us some sunshine and warm weather."

"Did he answer?" I asked.

She smiled. "I think he said 'Okay.' But he didn't say when or for how long."

2. Use your imagination. Visualize our winter snowscape as a return of the white-capped waves of the interior ocean that covered our state eons ago. Only now it's frozen. What might be in or under those endless waves of snow if they were really ocean? Spring could be upon us by the time we worked our way through this one.

3. Change your attitude. (Since you can't change the weather.) Our Constitution does guarantee an inalien-

Statue of Sacajawea with child appears to roam among frost laden trees on Central Wyoming College campus in Riverton.

Author's photo

Hoar frost feathers tree limbs in February.

Author's photo

able right to pursue happiness. You can chase it if you want, but I've always suspected this line was a constitutional chuckle inserted by some white-wigged forefather who'd worked overtime on that otherwise amazing document.

I'm not alone in this view. Humorist Ashley Brilliant asks, "Should I hurry to catch up with happiness? Or is happiness behind me hoping I'll slow down?"

Since we can't be happy without our own approval, I decided long ago that happiness is an attitude, a way of looking at life. So I'm putting winter in its place as writer Albert Camus did when he wrote, "In the depth of winter I finally learned that there was in me an invincible summer."

4. Confront it. Not all of us have such a choice. But many do, and age doesn't stop them. My husband Ned takes 80-year-old friends snowmobiling. They have a great time.

Our community provides many activities to help counteract winter doldrums. Sometimes it's a bit hard to convince myself I want to go somewhere enough to confront the weather. But once I'm out there, I'm glad I went.

5. Run away from home. Some winters I come close to considering such action. Then I turn on the television. I hear of tornadoes, floods, train collisions and avalanches. But not here.

Maybe such winters are meant to remind us of the unique diversity that calls to us here: hardy, colorful people; varied seasons, patterns and textures; nature's secrets and surprises. Isn't it awesome?

BROOKS LAKE SURPRISE

When patterns are broken, new worlds can emerge.
- Tuli Kupferberg

Ice on Brooks Lake in late June? That's Wyoming. Our first fishing trip to high country in the spring often brings surprises, but we've never seen this before. As of June 23, Brooks Lake Campground is still inaccessible. Huge snowbanks block the road.

My determined outdoor man decides we'll try Pinnacle Campground, up the hill a bit but near the good fishing. With the little travel trailer in tow, he engages the pickup's 4-wheel-drive and plows through several smaller drifts as we head up the hill. Soon that road too is blocked with snow, so we back into the parking spot just below it.

A wide stream of melt from the snowbank that claims the entire road above us flows directly in front of our doorstep. Ned grabs a shovel and directs the water to a different route, which frees the stream and me too. Not having to step out of the trailer into ice water certainly adds to my sense of liberty.

Brooks Lake is unbelievable. Except for thawed areas around the edges, the lake is still covered with breaking ice! Remember the song, "Old Buttermilk Sky?" That's what comes to mind - "Buttermilk Ice."

One spring when Brooks Lake was beginning to thaw, we watched in horror as a deer walked out onto the unstable ice, clearly bent on crossing. Several times her hooves broke through. Each time, she floundered then regained her footing and moved on. We stared, hearts pounding and almost in tears, expecting we'd have to watch the beautiful creature go under the ice and drown. There was simply no way we could help.

Eventually, the doe made it across the lake. But we've often wondered why she was so determined to take that treacherous route instead of going around.

Brooks Lake on June 23, still mostly covered with "buttermilk ice"

Author's photo

A cow moose leads her newborn calf across fast-flowing Brooks Lake Creek in spring thaw.

Ned Case photo

June 24: Much of the ice has disappeared, yet great floes still move across the lake and back again in tune with the ever changing winds. Casting a fish line onto the ice and letting it slide off the edge seems a great idea until we realize the softening ice only grabs the hook and hangs on.

At night, we sleep between flannel sheets and several blankets. Mornings and evenings, I pull on a turtleneck and a sweatshirt. That's inside the trailer, with a winter coat outdoors.

Despite the chill and heavy morning frost, a few brave flowers grace the greening hillsides - tiny wild alyssum, marsh marigolds and lots of dandelions. The willows are just starting to bloom with the little fuzzy gray catkins that I love.

Shortly after casting our fishing lines in the early morning, a pair of playful otters come swimming up the creek and into the lake. They climb onto the ice floes to sun themselves a while, then dive back into the water, making snorting sounds all the while. Maybe the sound is laughter. They seem to be having such fun.

June 25 - After fishing a while, we move the trailer down to Falls Campground just off the highway, seeking warmer weather so Ned can cook steaks outside on the grill. The steaks are great, but when I realize I'm gobbling my food because I'm so cold, it's time to move inside.

Most of the snow disappeared in a few days after we left, but El Nino, La Nina or something certainly made late June different this year.

Back home, someone asks, "But did you catch any fish?" Sure we did. "How many?" Enough. "What size?" They just fit in the cooler. "How big a cooler?" Enough questions. Why do you think coolers are available in so many different sizes?

BUILDING FORT FIZZLE

Well done is better than well said.   - *Benjamin Franklin*

"The water's in the ditch!" I sing out happily each spring. And I start scanning the newspapers to see how we're coming at building our own Fort Fizzle. The process began many years ago.

When the warming sun brings snowmelt from the shining blue mountains to nurse our thirsty land, it's like the milk of a mother's breast to the newborn. Most residents came to this Wind River Valley from dryland areas of other states. Yet we've grown so accustomed to this precious life-giving fluid that we often take it for granted.

While controversy flairs among claimants to its use for irrigation, the big waterways touch us in many ways, some dramatic, some humorous. All affect Wyoming lives as the history of the races grows, intertwined.

When we visited the Lolo Trail in Montana a few years ago, we read the fascinating and funny story of Fort Fizzle. It left a dent in my memory and a smile of hope in my heart.

In 1876, the story goes, a great battle was anticipated between the whites and the Nez Perce Indians to claim a section of the Lolo Trail. Apparently, neither really wanted to fight about it.

On the expected day of conflict, the white volunteers from the Bitterroot Valley decided to believe the Indians' promise to cooperate and went home. The Nez Perce didn't care to fight, either, and peacefully skirted the area to camp on down the trail. The anticipated but deserted spot of confrontation is humorously known to history as "Fort Fizzle."

Ever since visiting that area, I've thought about the ongoing disagreement over water in our valley and wondered if we could create our own Fort Fizzle. In my heart, I believe the Great Spirit provides the water for all life. That precious liquid already serves people of several races in Wyoming in more ways than we could imagine.

The canal that ran between the road and my first Wyoming home spawned all sorts of events besides the hatching of mosquitos. One year my father saved our crops from a hungry army of fat golden-brown crickets by rolling barrels of tractor fuel to the bridge that spanned the canal. With spigots opened just enough to drip an oily cover over the water, the marching hordes were repelled. An entire year's crop was saved.

I suspect my father also viewed the canal as a moat of sorts, when his daughters were dating age. The gradually sinking bridge which wasn't replaced until all his daughters married seemed just the right test of a young man's courage and determination.

A "dig" when waterways are dry in winter could unearth any number of treasures. I know a high school boy's class ring lies at the bottom of one. Since he made the mistake of dating both my sisters and I, the ring ended up in deep water one day when two of us were arguing over which one he really wanted to wear it.

Today, tubs and showers grace most if not all rural homes in this valley, but many young men of the 1930s and 40s took their baths in the irrigation canals in summer. After the first few shivers and gasps, the water could be tolerated and seemed to make more sense than carrying water in and out of the old galvanized tub.

Youngsters of that era also learned to swim in the canals. But the deep and swift-flowing waters were dangerous. Several good swimmers drowned in the canals, as did pet dogs. No life could survive the whirling suction of the big concrete drops.

Today, most of the canals have been placed underground. But there's still some disagreement between white irrigators and the nearby reservation residents as to how the water might be divided to serve us all.

Writer-artist Ashleigh Brilliant seems to be speaking to everyone involved with a sketch of an Indian chief who says, "Not even a great leader can get very far without great people to lead."

So what is "great?"

"Remarkable," says the dictionary. "Of noble character."

Our leaders could be brown, tan, white, red, or some other color if they can show us they're truly great, remarkable or noble enough to care equally for the welfare of all. As for the rest of us, if we see ourselves and each other as part of the human family and capable of being great people, we might all become just that. But we need a vision first, a vision of something like our own "Fort Fizzle."

We're working on it. As of this writing, we're almost there.

Meanwhile, when it's spring in Wyoming, the life-giving water flows down once more from its mountain birthplace to nurture our land. And while we may have conflicting ideas about "rights," we all agree on one thing: This precious resource deserves great respect as well as a springtime cheer. "The water's in the ditch!"

A SIMPLE MORNING HIKE?

In the right light, at the right time, everything is extraordinary
- Aaron Rose

You might expect spring morning hikes to be energizing and inspiring. They are that, and more. You never know what surprises lie out there waiting for you. That's part of the appeal.

After a wild Saturday night rain and hail storm, Ned and I started our Sunday morning trek around the driving range of the golf course behind our home. The deep blue mountains stood in the distance, still snow-capped, awesome and beautiful. Fresh clean air fed our lungs. A cloud of fog moved with us for a while, intent, I felt sure, on steaming my hair from curls to frizz just before church.

Suddenly, out of the fog came a strange sight: A herd of cattle guided by three llamas making their way across the driving range, apparently moving up from a morning drink at the Wind River below to higher pastures. A few days before, we'd watched 15 head of mule deer choose a similar trail.

We don't play golf, but to watch the sun and moon rise over that huge open field of green with all its surprises is indeed a glorious sight from our kitchen window.

This morning, we'd hiked down the path only a short way when Ned discovered the street was scattered with treasure, that view of course depending on what you covet. Everywhere we looked, eight to ten-inch night crawlers wriggled to get off the fast-drying pavement and into cool soil. Ned ran back to the garage for his bait box. Just happened he had a Monday fishing trip scheduled. How lucky can a man be?

Did I help pick up the big squirmy worms? Well, yes. Have you ever noticed how they tickle your palms when you hold them? Or how difficult they are to pick up after several have coated your hands with slime? (You have to be sensitive to the learning opportunities inherent in such activity to truly find your heart in it.)

A man we met eyed Ned's bait box and asked with a smile, "Having any luck?"

"Some," said Ned. "But I'm more concerned about the luck I'll need tomorrow."

Soon we met a man with a big dog. The man carried an unattached leash in his hand. We greeted one another as we met with the usual nod and polite "hello" one issues strangers.

The second we passed, a huge body slammed against my back and shoulders, knocking me to the ground. Ned tried to catch me, but failed. I heard the sharp order, "Heel!" and the leash was quickly snapped in place.

"Why don't you keep that animal leashed if he attacks people?" I screamed in fright and anger, my knee and elbow bruised and aching.

"Oh, I'm sorry, ma'am," the man said. "But he didn't attack you. He was just playing."

"I don't call that play," I retorted. "Strange how such logic comes so brightly to the one who isn't flat on the ground."

I've always loved animals. I was raised a country girl, so I try to learn from them. I'm quite sure physical contact from behind is generally known as "stalking" in the animal world.

Later, I phoned our trusted veterinarian to ask why the dog might behave as he did. He warned that all dogs have the potential to attack at any time and that city laws require dogs be leashed when out of their own yards for that reason.

It was a frightening experience, but I don't give up easily. I plan to heal my fear with more early morning hikes. I'll continue to listen for the music of meadow larks and robins, the call of sandhill cranes and yips of coyotes down by the river. I'll let the fragrance of pink and white blossoms tease my nose and watch for pleasant surprises like the curious "hail banks" we found along the path that Sunday morning. And yes, I'll expect more deer and other wild creatures to make use of the beautiful pine strewn grassy area called a "driving range" by humans and seen as something quite different by animals.

No, I'm not about to give up hiking. Nature's therapy for the unpleasant part of my experience that morning awaits. I wonder if it includes helping Ned pick up more night crawlers?

THE FISHING SYNDROME

When the fish are biting, no problem in the world is big enough to be remembered.   *- O.A. Battista*

On a morning hike my mate relays this bit of wisdom, "When a man decides to go fishing, nothing in the world can stop him."

I smile. "Really?"

Actually, I've been aware of this peculiar syndrome for some time. I just didn't know he recognized it.

After breakfast, he says nonchalantly, "Guess I'll go fishing today. Want to go?"

I stare at the mountains shrouded in threatening dark clouds. "It's storming up there. Doesn't look like fishing weather to me."

"It'll clear up," he says in a confident tone.

Why am I hearing, "Neither rain nor hail nor dark of night?"

Against my better judgment, I pack a lunch, pull on my old jeans and hiking boots. We jump in the pickup truck and head for high country. As we near Brooks Lake the clouds are beginning to break and drift. I see a faraway look in his eyes.

"Better wear rubber boots," he says. "We'll be wading creeks and sloughs all day."

Did you ever try to hike in rubber boots? They slide all over your feet and beat on your toes. You feel like a construction worker whose jackhammer slipped.

We head out, leaving our lunch in the pickup to eat when we return. The miles move under our boots. Wildflowers wave from the hillside. Mosquitoes feast on our bodies, along with some tiny flea-type bugs that leave an itch like Oklahoma chiggers.

My man hikes on to Upper Brooks Lake while I fish the creek below. After a couple of hours he returns.

"Get any fish?" he asks.

"Three," I say.

"I got nine brookies - about 12 inchers."

It's time to whip my prize out of the creel. "A rainbow 16 inches long," I crow. "Got it in a still pool just beyond the falls."

Strange. He looks as pleased as if he'd caught it himself. Then I remember. I got it in the very pool he told me to try.

We begin our trek back over the miles of meadow. The rubber boots slip, slide and rub on tired feet.

"My toes hurt," I lament. "I can hardly walk."

"Mine too," he says. "Try curling your toes."

"They're so stiff and sore they can't curl," I reply.

"Might help to trim our toenails," he says.

By now I'm getting hungry, thirsty and weary. About halfway down the hill, I hear him say, "Let's sit on that log over there. I've got a Snickers in my pocket."

My mouth waters. "Might help us get on down the hill."

We reach the log. He sits down, yanks off his boot, pulls a nail clipper from his pocket and proceeds to trim his toenails.

"Where's the candy bar?" I ask.

"What candy bar?"

"The Snickers! The one you said you had in your pocket."

"I didn't say 'Snickers.' I said 'snipper.'"

I gulp the last bit of saliva that might bathe my parched throat. My stomach growls.

I trim my toenails and pull on my boots. My feet feel better, but it's a poor substitute for a candy bar.

Back at the pickup truck we drink the water jug dry and gobble a sandwich.

At home that evening, eating popcorn in my easy chair I'm thinking only of my big catch as the words of

O.A. Battista run through my mind: "When the fish are biting, no problem in the world is big enough to be remembered."

And I hear the mountain's call . . . . .

TO CAPTURE A RAINBOW

I've always regarded nature as the clothing of God.
- Alan Hovhaness

At beautiful Brooks Lake above Dubois one morning, I looked out our trailer window to see a small, familiar looking elderly man in blue jeans, denim jacket and an old hat, ambling down to the lake to watch the fog lift from the water.

I rubbed my eyes and stared. From a distance the man looked startlingly like my father. But my father died years ago. I let my imagination wander. If he were ever to return to Earth, I thought, he'd most likely appear at Brooks Lake, a spot he and my mother loved nearly as much as their Wyoming farm.

It was a haunting experience. I discovered I didn't want to see the man closer, didn't want to learn his identity. He might disappoint me by turning into someone else. It seemed better to fancy my father might have strolled in with the morning mist.

"Imagination will often carry us to worlds that never were," wrote the eminent scientist Carl Sagan. "But without it we go nowhere."

And yet, as David Gates once wrote in *Newsweek* magazine, "When it comes to wonder, beauty and mystery, fantasy is a pale imitation of the real world."

My father led us to know both views.

Visiting in my parents' home one summer, Ned and I watched my father go to the kitchen and pop a vitamin E capsule into his mouth with a mischievous grin.

"I need to live one more day," he explained.

His gaze moved toward the mountains. Their call that day was undeniable. We packed a picnic lunch, gathered our fishing gear and headed for Brooks Lake.

There, where the mountains climbed high all around us, we slid our boat into the water. Near the center of the lake, we cast our lines and settled back to await the thrilling tug of a fish. Several low puffy clouds moved in and sprinkled us down, then drifted slowly toward the pinnacles.

Soon a vibrant, sun-kissed rainbow appeared, so near it seemed we could reach out and touch it. The rainbow arched itself perfectly over a green curve of pines with the lofty rock peaks behind them, in a color contrast and placement one could never have imagined.

While Ned struggled to catch the glory on film without upsetting the boat, we watched in awe as the arc hovered and glowed. Slowly it separated into small misty forms that lifted and crept away to the crevices of the pinnacles like mischievous children caught dipping into their mother's colorful cosmetics.

But rainbows aren't often captured, and we didn't manage to catch this one except in memory and imagination.

Back home that night, as we relived the haunting experience my father remarked humbly, "There was need to live for this day, wasn't there?"

He knew now it wasn't a joke. Yet without his imaginative morning comment to stir our thoughts as to what the day might hold, we'd have missed a rare and treasured experience.

Maybe that's why he seemed to appear to me in the morning mist years later. Maybe I needed him to remind me to watch for the rainbow, to remember, "There is need to live for this day."

PART IV

WILDLIFE

Getting to Know You -

Animal or human, colorful, spirited creatures inhabit Wyoming's hills and valleys. These stories reveal traits common to both, while allowing wildlife to share those uniquely their own.

IN THE EYES OF BEHOLDERS

We usually see the things we are looking for - so much so that we sometimes see them where they are not. — *Eric Hoffer*

Ever since childhood, I've felt a pang when I hear someone described as "homely." I always wonder what is meant. Homely? Compared to what or whom? Who may judge?

On a wagon ride to observe the elk at the National Winter Refuge in Jackson Hole, our guide pointed out an animal whose horns grew in an unusual downward direction, closer to his eyes than his ears. Visitors aboard the wagon stared, commented and wondered. All grew silent when a father said softly to his small daughter, "See? We can't all be perfect."

That weird rack of horns could probably be termed "genetic accident." Strangely, the same words could explain what's called "natural beauty" in humans.

My father had his own view of all this. If we children criticized our looks, he'd growl as if personally offended, "Fits your face, doesn't it?" As if he'd planned each of us feature by feature. Or maybe he just wanted us to be glad we had the right things in the right places.

Abe Lincoln is often described as a homely man. In childhood, and yet today, I pore over one history book after another hunting for a photograph of Lincoln that makes me see him as anything other than a very special man. Homeliness wasn't even a part of him, to my sight.

As is my habit, I turn to the animal kingdom to test my own honesty of attitude, to seek the unvarnished truth. I find it in a willow patch in the Wind River mountains, in the form of a big cow moose.

Her coarse, rough-coated body with long head and drooping nose almost dare me to proclaim her beauty. Yet she isn't fazed by what I see, so long as I stay out of her greening gold and red willows. I must confess my first reaction comes close to viewing her as a less than attractive creation.

Then I remember one of her kind who stood quietly for Ned to photograph on an early Brooks Lake morning. He got a wonderful silhouette of her standing at water's edge. The background of blue mirror water, green trees, and pinnacles rising into the clouds completed the picture as if it were posed.

We had the photograph enlarged and decorated the foreground with dried mountain flowers and grasses for a longtime friend, Eldon (Jonesie) Jones, who'd owned the Basketeria Grocery in the small Wyoming town where we attended high school. Jonesie had explored the Wyoming mountains and appreciated the wildlife they nurtured as much as anyone could.

We took the framed photograph to Jonesie's bedside where he lay ill with bone cancer. His blue eyes welled with tears.

"You mean you kids did this just for me?" he asked in wonder.

As if time hadn't touched us. As if we'd brought him the moon.

It was such a small gesture on our part. But Jonesie saw that old moose as beautiful. Ever since, I've thought she was too. If God made any homely creatures to live on this earth, I doubt that He knows it.

Cow moose catches her breath in the shade of a golden willow tree at Pheasant Crest Farm.

Ned Case photo

A MOOSE ON MIDVALE

Life is at its best when it's shaken and stirred. - F. Paul Facult

"There's a - a - wild animal!" I screamed.

The sight of a cow moose charging through the back yard between the house and garage of a Midvale farm must surely excuse my reaction. The auditory assault brought Ned to a sudden standing position from his desk barely two feet away.

Just then a pickup truck roared into our yard and out jumped a breathless, tousle-haired big man in his sock feet yelling, "Get a picture! Get a picture!"

Ned looked out the back door. "Yup. It's a wild animal," he declared.

I looked from the moose to the man, still blinking my eyes.

Ned grabbed his camera and proceeded to stalk the moose who'd cleared a couple of fences and taken refuge behind a row of tall willow trees. Our three horses galloped to the fence corner to stare, necks erect and nostrils flared. The poor winded moose hung her head and gasped for breath. After two or three deep drags of oxygen, she lifted her long nose and sped off across the hayfield.

Wild creatures are moving in closer these days. The day of the moose visit, we'd just returned from a trek down in the field to observe three handsome buck deer when she arrived. Great horned owls have raised young in our yard twice in the past three years. Little red foxes are everywhere. Often we see them crossing the road or searching the fields for mice or rabbits - or heaven forbid, our protected pheasants.

So many of the beautiful birds live in this area that when we came here we decided to name our new/old farm "Pheasant Crest." Inspired, I painted a large colorful bird with a long tail to proclaim our pheasant refuge. Ned

Cow moose streaks through the yard at Pheasant Crest Farm.

Ned Case photo

erected the symbol out near the road and dutifully tacked "No Hunting" signs to the fenceposts. We listened for pheasant calls and rejoiced in our own wild roosters announcing the dawns and sunsets.

We enjoy watching the foxes, but they're hard on our pheasant population. One day Ned asked solemnly, "What will we name our place if the foxes devour all our birds?"

"Don't worry," I said, "I've already sketched a little red critter with a big fluffy tail. We'll simply switch from "Pheasant Crest" to "Fox Ridge Farm.""

I don't think he was pacified. But I tried.

Meanwhile, we like to believe the wayward moose got a good night's rest under our trees then found her way to the Owl Creek Mountains where a welcoming clan hailed her arrival.

WHEN CONFRONTING A COUGAR

So many tangles in life are ultimately hopeless that we have no appropriate sword other than laughter.   - Gordon W. Allport

Wyoming is cougar country. A television spot once offered advice from those in the know on how to deal with the big cats if we should happen to come upon one. Or if one of them should come upon us. I wonder if our television friends might consider a "show and tell" lesson for this little scaredy-cat? You'll soon see why I need extra guidance.

"Remain standing and fight back," is the well-meant advice offered this day. The likelihood of my being able to respond successfully is small. So am I. I pull myself to my full height of 5'1" and proceed to bone up on the matter.

My internet encyclopedia tells me a full grown male cougar/mountain lion/puma, "from tip of nose to tip of tail can measure as long as nine feet. The tail is about one third the total length." That leaves six feet of real cat. His body would be a foot longer than mine. Right off, I recognize trouble. Male lions get to eat first.They probably prefer tender human females.

"The cougar commonly stalks its prey without making a sound, then springs 20 to 60 feet to pounce on it," I read. How can I remain standing when a cat weighing as much as 160 pounds has the advantage of such momentum and has already planned his supper? I feel like a bison at the buffalo jump.

Unless I have a gun and am allowed to use it, how in the world might I fight back? A stick? A walking cane? And where's kitty's vulnerable spot in case I'm still on my feet at this point and able to wield my weapon?

"Remain standing and fight back." The words race through my mind.

Should I despair of such counsel and consider diving into the safe waters of a nearby stream, I'm now advised the puma does not hesitate to swim wide rivers.

He's strictly carnivorous and requires large quantities of meat to satisfy his great appetite. Surely, he wouldn't bother with me. I'd provide only a couple of quick gulps. But my source has more information.

"While it may bring down such large animals as elk and moose, the mountain lion does not disdain the tiniest mice as food." So much for safety in small servings like me.

Not one to give up easily, suppose I happen to have a pocket knife on me. My arm's short, I'm right-handed, and that shoulder has already dealt with rotator cuff surgery.

I read on. "The cougar has a special taste for porcupines, which it manages to kill and eat without running afoul of the quills."

What ever made me fancy that brandishing a small knife might put fear into the soul of that big cat, anyway? My fingernails can't even get a knife blade out of its slot. And how do you suppose the cougar's entertaining himself while I'm trying to get my knife operative?

"The puma is discreet, but no coward. It fights on even terms with the wolverine and the jaguar, and more often than not is the victor," my electronic book of wisdom continues.

"Remain standing and fight back."

In case I still am and still can, what do I try next? Strangle him with my belt or boot string? And what about the lion now? Is he quietly marveling at my resourcefulness as I bend to undo a boot string or belt?

Hoping to look at this somewhat lightly but not in ignorance, I consult my friend Herb Burden, a longtime Wyoming lion hunter.

"Well, a good bluff is always better than a poor fight," drawls Herb. "You can't outrun a cougar. So a club or rock is certainly worth the try." Then he chuckles. "Of course a big hound and a gun are best."

That's what I was afraid of. How close would I have to be to zap the cougar with my pepper spray when he springs?

In my mind I feel the rush of air as the big cat comes flying my way. He slams into my body. I hear a deep gasp . . .

Guess who got the pepper spray?

I like and admire all species of felines. They're graceful and sure-footed where I'm often not. I know I could learn from them. But please, guys, if I'm to confront them, could I have a little more information on the battle plan?

OPEN YOUR EYES TO THE PRAIRIES

Let a joy keep you. Reach out your hands and take it when it runs by
                                                    - Carl Sandburg

The flowering crab trees and lilacs that grace our home-town are breathtaking in spring. Of course, I have a 2 or 3-week headache about the time all this begins, but I'm refusing to blame it on any part of nature's performance. In fact, I can really get high on a spring drive.

On a warm sunny day we drive out Sand Draw Road, hoping to see antelope fawns through the binoculars. We've learned to expect the first ones June 1, but occasionally a mother antelope just can't wait one more day. This time, on May 31, we see our first fawns of the year, a pair of tiny brown twins dancing around their mother in the fresh green grass.

Driving down a side-road, we see a fox kit, 12 or 14 inches long, dart back into his den after inspecting the meadowlark a parent has dropped off at the door. We linger awhile, thinking he probably just can't wait to come out and taste the bird.

He can and does outwait us. We get out of the car to examine his home. At the far end of the long culvert lies a kangaroo rat. No food shortage in this home.

We drive on, almost overwhelmed at the wildflower population on Wyoming prairies. Indian paintbrush grows everywhere. Pushing up through the gray-green sagebrush, the vivid bracts make the sage seem abloom with bright red, orange, pink or yellow blossoms.

I learn from my agronomist mate that paintbrush is a parasite. It must have an underground connection with roots of some other plant from which to steal at least a part of its food. If you try to transplant it to your garden, you'll be unlikely to get the host plant with it and it will die.

Scattered over a small, dry area of hillside, we find lovely tufted evening primrose in bloom. The large flowers, about 2-1/2 inches across, are rose-colored and delicate. They last only a short time and resemble a bit of twisted pink tissue paper as they wilt.

Other prairie flowers in bloom are white daisies, purple and pink asters, purple-blue penstemmon, lupine, purple and white vetch and other varieties, along with a host of tiny yellow, white and blue-blossomed flowers whose names I haven't yet learned.

On our return, we stop by the little red fox's lair to see if he has cleaned up his plate. The yellow-breasted meadowlark still lies on its back at one end of the culvert. I run to the other end to find the kangaroo rat gone.

"Not surprising," says Ned when I report my findings. "I'd think the rat would be better eating than the bird."

"I'd rather eat a meadowlark," I comment. "But you traveled on a company expense account for years. You probably know gourmet when you see it."

He doesn't seem to think this quite as funny as I do.

All nonsense aside, it's an exciting place out there. Everyone should experience a slow drive across Wyoming's prairie land in the spring. And when you do, keep your eyes open!

Owlets on tree limb at Pheasant Crest Farm, friendly and fearless.
Ned Case photo

LORDS OF DARKNESS

The universe is full of magical things patiently waiting for our wits to grow sharper. — *Eden Phillpotts*

It was early March when Ned dashed in to announce, "The great horned owl is nesting."

That's usually one of the first signs of spring in rural Wyoming. The hatchings generally occur early in April, an event we keenly anticipate when none of the mares are foaling and the cat is spayed.

The nesting owls first caught our attention one year when Ned started up his chainsaw to cut a dead elm tree. The raucous sound brought an owl hen flapping from her lofty nest in the elm. The woodcutting halted abruptly and the lumberjack exchanged his saw for a camera.

When two hatchlings appeared, standing over-sized in their nest like huge puffs of white cotton, four dark-blotched eyes peered down. We were instantly and permanently mesmerized. Ned stood a 20-foot ladder against the elm and climbed up to snap a picture. Mama owl departed to a nearby tree and hooted at her babes who quickly hunkered down in the nest about 40 feet above the ladder.

Ned descended. "I'm afraid she'll desert her young now," he worried. "Some birds do. Wish I'd stayed away."

I couldn't help the mental picture that hit me. "I can see you now, climbing that tall ladder several times a day carrying a couple of mice by the tails, then shinnying up the rest of the way to feed your hungry orphans," I teased.

But the owl mom did return. After that, we watched the family with binoculars, recording their behavior in memory and wishing we had a telephoto lens for the camera.

When the chicks left the nest, they sat on nearby branches, exercising and stretching the absurdly long,

Owlet on ground and unable to fly, glares at cat and puffs feathers to enlarge image.

Ned Case photo

unfeathered wings. At the base of their tree lay mouse heads, magpie feathers and a muskrat tail, all remnants of the goodies the parent owls had brought to support the rushing growth of their young.

Later, when they'd grown feathers to help them fly, the fledglings moved to low hanging branches of a huge cottonwood tree. There we were allowed to come very close and they sat almost like pets, sometimes winking one eye, sometimes silently ogling us as we did them. Often, they lay like beanbags tossed over a branch, slumped and dozing.

Soon we began to hear strange little squawks at night as they practiced trying to hoot like their parents. The attemps were crude and gutteral, sounding as if they were in desperate need of a speech therapist. By autumn they could hoot and fly like proper owls and disappeared from our area.

Once we found an owl chick sitting on a tree stump, apparently blown from the nest by a strong wind. Still down-covered and lacking wing feathers, it was unable to fly. The next morning, I spied the chick between the house and garage with Mariah, the cat, crouched nearby. Hurriedly, I began planning my rescue strategy. But the baby owl beat me to it.

Stretching its body to an imposing display of height, it fluffed its feathers, or rather, fluffed its fluff and glared, larger then life and now nearly twice the size of the cat. Mariah, overwhelmed by the strange metamorphosis, backed away in a wide circle and came slinking to me for protection. The owlet waddled nonchalantly across the yard to the willow trees, much like a slow moving duck.

Each year, a pair of owls nests here. Some people fear them, but we enjoy the eerie sounds of these lords of darkness as they glide in on hushed wings at dusk. We like to study the quiet mystery of our professor-like friends in feathery coats. But I wonder why they choose this spot?

Then I step inside our house. Three photos of the owlets hang on the wall. A ceramic owl holds a pot scrubber at the sink. Even the canisters Ned gave me years ago are owls. Can it be the big birds simply feel welcome here?

A HUNTING LESSON

A human being's first responsibility is to shake hands with himself.
                                                    - Henry Winkler

This was not your average hunting lesson and I learned nothing about handling a gun. In fact, I'm almost afraid to touch one. Nevertheless, the experience was profound.

That fall as we drove Flagstaff Road in the Wind River Mountains pickup trucks roared by one after another, loaded with evidence of successful elk and moose hunts. A couple in a pickup truck stopped us. The driver rolled down his window.

"Seen any moose along this road?" he asked.

"No. Are you a moose hunter?" Ned asked.

"Sure am," the man declared. "And I'm really hunting them!"

He was serious. So was the woman beside him. When they drove on, I chuckled.

"Apparently it's his first time at big game hunting," I said. "He must have thought the moose would be lining the road waiting for him."

Surely, I reasoned, anyone planning to find big game would expect to hike or ride a horse back into the timber a way.

Two weeks later, Ned went antelope hunting with a friend. Because of a tragic snowmobile accident years before, this man can barely walk with the aid of two canes. He suffers great pain, yet does not allow self-pity. Nature calls to him loud and clear and he participates in every way he can. Because of his disability he is permitted to shoot from his vehicle, the only possible way he could share in the event. A crack marksman, he quickly brought down his game that day.

When Ned and the friend's wife got the animal back to the vehicle, this man, strong and capable except for his ambulatory problem, dropped to the ground and deftly assisted in dressing out and loading the meat. Ned was awed. And since Ned didn't have a license, our friend insisted on giving him a hind quarter of the meat.

Reflecting on the experience later, I was hit with a startling thought: If one were to meet our friend driving down the road, one would see only the ready grin, the husky shoulders and a healthy tan. That's all I saw of the man on Flagstaff Road.

Now, instead of laughs, I felt a lump in my throat and tears in my eyes. It's a lesson I value deeply. That Thanksgiving and this, I'm grateful I can walk. But even more, I'm thankful for people who remind the rest of us, without saying a word, that the ability to make the best of whatever life hands us may be the greatest blessing of all

INTREPID CREATURES

We don't know who we are until we see what we can do.
- Martha Grimes

It's interesting to observe the birds who remain in Wyoming in winter to tough it out with the rest of us. An eagle soaring through a cold blue sky or a pheasant crowing from a snowy woodpile touch me aesthetically, maybe because they're elusive.

In birds that allow a closer look, I see human characteristics as they fuss, party, or behave with confusion and skepticism. Sometimes, they and we clearly define the negative use of the term "birdbrain."

On full-mooned autumn nights, we're often wakened by a pair of great horned owls sweeping down into the tall trees near our house. First we hear the male's deep-voiced hoot, then the female's gentle mimic of his cry. At times, their calls collide noisily. This is always followed by the silent treatment. Finally, the female initiates communication as if ill-timed response could only have been her error. The male doesn't hoot again until she does.

I suppose you've never seen humans in these roles, similar or reversed?

One year, our renter grew malting (beer) barley. On a winter evening, a small nephew burst into the house shouting for us to come look.

"Well, hurry," he urged. "It's amazing!"

He had the right word. Barely skimming the tops of our giant cottonwoods, hundreds of Canada geese came gliding in from Ocean Lake, stitching the skies with their graceful "V." Daily, the huge birds returned for happy hour on the barley left in the fields after harvest. A hike along the edge of the field provided a good view as they nodded, chatted and jostled for service, like customers at the Beer Barley Lounge in an old western movie.

One day, I watched a lone goose arrive and settle in a grain field. Assuming he was on a reconnaissance trip, I waited and watched for the rest of his party. After about 15 minutes, he upped his long periscope neck, looked about as if he'd suddenly realized he had no following and flew off in a honking panic. Somehow, I was reminded of a politician who only fancies himself a great leader.

We also discovered that air disasters occur in the avian world as in ours. Apparently their navigators miscalculate, too.

Returning from town one winter evening, we were startled to see colorful mallard ducks scattered over a section of Eight Mile Road. The poor creatures seemed stunned. We stopped and tried to get them to move. They wouldn't. Or couldn't. Finally, we drove on slowly, darting this way and that to avoid hitting them. Since the air hung heavy with frosty fog and they weren't far from their Ocean Lake home, we wondered if they'd somehow lost their sense of direction. Or maybe the dark strip of road was perceived by their guide as water in the dense, foggy night.

Whatever the reason for their strange disorientation, when we drove to the airport early next morning, all had, sadly, been hit by vehicles or died from the hard landing on or along the road.

Woodpeckers, hawks, magpies and ravens make up most of the remainder of dauntless birds that winter in Wyoming. Ravens, the raggedy carrion feeders, serve a useful purpose. But I get other messages from the ominous looking birds. When we first began remodeling our old house, I noticed a raven watching me from a post as I whisked off to town for building materials one day. Maybe Edgar Allen Poe impressed me too deeply in childhood, but I was sure the raven shook his head and croaked a pessimistic "Nevermore" as he eyed our remodeling attempts.

But the raven only roused the fighting side of me. Perhaps that's how we and other tough birds deal with Wyoming winters. Challenge simply provides a reason to prove what we're made of. At the same time, it reveals a similarity of feisty, intrepid character that seems common to all creatures who winter here.

SPRING BREAK

To acquire knowledge, one must study; to acquire wisdom, one must observe.   - Marilyn vos Savant

"Spring break." The term meant little to us. Then, after years in liaison work between industry and colleges, my mate retired. Quickly bored with that, he rejoined the academic world to videotape classes at our community college. "Spring break" took on new life. Suddenly it was imperative that we kick loose, go somewhere, do something wild and crazy to celebrate this pre-spring hiatus.

Lest readers envision something like flying off to Florida, lying topless on the beach, drinking beer and staying up all night for a week, here's the reckless proposition I heard.

"We could rent a motel room in Dubois, snowmobile a while, go to Jackson for lunch, snowmobile on Togwotee Pass and come back to the motel."

While your imagination is dealing with all this, you can substitute my mate rubbing painkilling cream on my shoulders in Dubois for the suntan-lotion-in-Florida scene.

And the "wild life" I mentioned earlier? It's a matter of interpretation. The Wyoming version has its own appeal.

In the Wind River Mountains we find foothill willows dotted with moose, coyotes loping across high country snowbanks, and deer raising long ears to attention as we slow to watch them graze.

Again, the romance in honoring spring's approach lies in the interpretation. A sleigh ride in the Jackson Hole National Elk Refuge heightens the heartbeat and lifts the spirit as we share with others from across the country the privilege of riding among 11,000 to 17,000 of the beautiful wild creatures on a warm, snow-thawing day.

Generally, the herd numbers between 9,000 to 11,000 elk. Though it sometimes happens, a 17,000 member feeding herd is considered far too large accord-

Elk at Jackson Hole feeding ground on stormy winter day.

Author's photo

ing to a joint agreement between the Wyoming Game and Fish Commission, the National Elk Refuge and Grand Teton National Park. An unusually warm autumn and minimum snowfall can greatly increase the herd size when hunters fail to harvest their usual numbers. If elk can't be tracked in snow, as any hunter knows, they're hard to find. But once in the refuge, they're cared for.

On this day, Jake, a half-Clydesdale, half-Shire horse and his Shire team-mate Barney prance along, taking our sleigh through slush and puddles, past a lone meadow tree where a handsome bald eagle quietly announces his lordship of the skies.

There's tension, too. Not a brawl like you might encounter at an out-of-control beach party, but Jake and Barney aren't always in agreement either. At a fast-flowing stream, the two big horses come to a defiant halt. No amount of coaxing or rein slapping by our young teamster can induce them to move.

Finally, the teamster steps down from the sleigh and speaks firm instructions directly into the big horses' ears. He resumes his seat and slaps the reins. We turn in a large arc and approach the stream from a new angle. A few tips and bumps and we're safely on the other side.

When we reach the huge elk herd happily munching on domestically grown hay with the majestic Tetons for a backdrop, visitors gasp and grab their cameras. The beauty of these thousands of wild creatures relying on man to help them survive cold Wyoming winters is awesome. The winter feeding program has been underway for 90 years.

Several coyotes slink warily about the perimeter of the elk herd as if they're guard dogs, there to protect.

Questions fly. Our pleasant and knowledgeable teamster provides ready answers.

"One hundred to one hundred fifty elk die of natural causes here in the refuge area each winter. That's why the coyotes are here."

"Antler points do not denote age as is commonly believed. Rather, the elk's incisor teeth have rings like trees that accurately tell their age."

"Mature bulls begin to shed their antlers about April 1. A pair of large antlers weighs 25 to 30 pounds."

When the antlers are shed, Boy Scouts are permitted to gather and market them to support their Scout programs. A huge stack of antlers marks the town square of Jackson, a favorite background for tourist photographers from every direction and nation.

Driving home, happily filled with wisdom and inspiration from the natural world, I'm struck with a simple but profound fact: Sometimes you go on "spring break" from an educational institution and keep on learning anyway.

And I ask myself, "Why would anyone go to Florida to welcome spring to Wyoming?"

NOT EVEN A MOUSE?

We do not remember days; we remember moments.
                                                    - Cesare Pavese

"Twas the night before Christmas and all through the house, not a creature was stirring–not even a mouse."

Sound kind of dull? Your Christmas needn't be like that. You can have a creature stirring. It's not easy, but with proper dedication to detail, this exciting experience can be yours. Here's how we did it.

We were sitting in the living room on a cold December afternoon when my peripheral vision caught a small phantom-like form darting along the floor molding.

"There's a mouse! A mouse!" I shouted, jumping to my feet.

"A mouse?" Ned asked, incredulous. Our house had just passed its third birthday. "How could a mouse get in?"

"I don't know, but it's here!"

The little gray rodent dashed from the shadows of one chair to the next.

"It IS a mouse!" Ned exclaimed.

I thought of the time he insisted the bear I saw was just an old tree stump. He eventually believed me that time, too.

He ran for the broom. For some reason I don't understand, it's his favorite weapon for dealing with a mouse. Was he going to try to sweep the mouse outdoors? Or smash it on the end of the broom I hold in my hands?

We chased the mouse into the bedroom. I wondered what I'd do with it if I caught it. The thought almost squelched any serious effort on my part. But what if it climbed in between the sheets with us at night?

Suddenly, the mouse disappeared. We'd had two pairs of eyes glued to that furry body, yet it had eluded us. We waited.

"Maybe it's hanging by its toenails to the back of the dresser," I offered.

Balancing that likelihood against the thought of lifting our big triple dresser, Ned flung me a sidewise glance and clutched the broom.

"By morning, it may give birth to a dozen more," I added.

"Guess I'd better go get some traps." He hurried downtown and returned with six mouse traps which we baited with cheese and set in closets and behind the dresser where the last sighting occurred. I cringed. What if I walked into a closet barefoot? I could almost feel those strong trap jaws closing on my big toe and hear a squeaky cackle bursting from a dark corner.

Preparing dinner that evening, I went to a back room closet for one of the sweet Walla Walla onions Ned grew in his garden last summer. As I sliced into the onion my brain lit up like a Christmas tree.

"Do you suppose that mouse was in the box of onions we brought in from the garage last night?" I asked. "Could we actually have moved a mouse into the house ourselves?"

We took the onion box outside and dumped it in the breezeway. Sure enough, at the bottom among the nice homey husks were numerous tiny mouse droppings!

The final word is the mouse met his demise the first day and we didn't see any more. So that Christmas eve we rejoiced that no creature was stirring. Especially a mouse.

FISHING: A MAN THING

All blessings are mixed blessings.   *- John Updike*

Father's Day will soon be here and I'd like to write something for the father of my son. But how can I do it now? We're in our little travel trailer in Wind River Canyon, overdosed on conventions - three in a row.

It feels quite homelike here despite the fact I have no computer to help me arrange my thoughts. On the table sits a small blue pottery vase filled with pink peonies, painted daisies and coral and yellow columbine from our yard at home. It's a tradition my mate began years ago: Always take a bit of home with you when you travel.

Our trailer sits on a bank high above the Wind River. Tall grasses frame the area and wave a warning of the dangerous precipice nearby.

This morning Ned rigs my fishing pole and fills a bait box for me before hurrying off down the river to test his own luck.

I gather my gear and pick my way gingerly down the steep path to the water, still wondering what I can write about Father's Day. I think of our son and remember the synonym finder he gave me one Mother's Day inscribed, "May you find something you haven't already said." That's what I'm looking for now - something that hasn't already been said about a man's special day. Maybe the answer is in the energy-filled water below. Maybe an idea will leap from the swirling eddies, like a fish after a fly. I toss out my line and wait.

Father's Day, hm-m-m? My dad loved to fish, as does the father of my son. Must be a man thing.

Hang on! My pole is bending. I grab it and start reeling in the line. Shortly, I've landed a small walleye. My throat tightens and tickles at the same time. I've never caught a walleye before. Already I'm feeling inspired. But where is the answer in this?

I rebait my hook with a large nightcrawler. Sure, he's wiggly and slimy and he doesn't like this big hook. But I want a big fish and it's my theory that big fish only bite on big worms.

I cast my line far out into the river's flow and wait . . and contemplate. . .

I turn to consider the steep hill behind me, lush with green grass 18 to 20 inches tall. Big rust-colored rocks jut up through the grass in colorful contrast. Redwing blackbirds flutter from bush to bush along water's edge, calling, "Chirr-r-r. Chirr-r-r." A raft with nine people aboard floats by. A freight train wails as it chugs out of a dark tunnel and rounds the bend.

Suddenly, my pole jumps and jiggles in lively action. I grab it and start reeling. The pole bends sharply and I reel harder, wondering if I have space to land this big fish without trading places with him. My catch, a fine rainbow, nears the shore fighting and jumping all the way. I slip on wet rocks and land hard on my rear. If I lose this big fish, I'll just die. . .

I pull him in and soon as I locate the hook, I shove my thumb through his gill and hang on, my heart pounding.

Shortly, my fishing partner appears, working his way down the hillside. He's carrying a big walleye by the gill. Without a word, he clips it onto the fish chain beside my rainbow.

His walleye is several inches longer.

It's all coming clear to me now. The inspiration for my writing did emerge from that energy-filled water. Not quite as I'd expected, but this one's for you, love. Happy Father's Day! I'm glad your fish was the biggest. Fishing is really a man thing, anyway.

Isn't it???

Fox kit emerges from sagebrush hiding place.

Ned Case photo

Curious fox kit moves closer to car.

Ned Case photo

RARE AND PERFECT DAYS IN JUNE

In all things of nature there is something of the marvelous.
                                                    - Aristotle

On June 1, we drove out into Wyoming country where green extended that year as far as the eye could see or miles could measure. We'd hoped to find new antelope fawns. The time was right, but this particular year we found none. Antelope does were plentiful, yet we didn't spot one with a babe at her side. Maybe they were simply hiding in the dense grass.

A week or so later, we tried again. That day, as Ned drove, I spotted movement just beyond the roadside fence.

"Wait, wait! There's something out there..."

He stopped the car. Rising from the lush grasses and blue-gray sage stood a sandy mound surrounded by watermelon-colored Indian Paintbrush.

A rusty head with a pointed nose and oversize dark ears emerged from the den. As we watched, another small fox kit bounded to the surface, then another and another. Their legs and feet were dark like their ears, almost black. Long full tails lent balance to the small bodies.

Binoculars gave a close-up view of the play that ensued. Ironically called "kits" when they look much more like pups, the four small creatures bounced, chased and frolicked while we watched.

Dozens of cars whizzed by, not one even slowing to wonder at what we preceived a rare sharing of the wild.

Finally, we saw the mother fox's head move where she watched from a dimple in the land not far away. Apparently she decided we were a bit too attentive to her family. We heard not a sound, but suddenly the babies disappeared into the sandy mound in a flash of red fur. The show was over.

Ned drove to the spot next morning with his camera. He got a few pictures, but by the time he arrived the next day with better distance equipment, the entire family had moved.

The following weekend we drove further into the area, hoping to see the foxes again. Under a lake-blue sky sailing small pillow clouds, we hiked up a hillside in the cool breeze to search for evening primrose we'd seen there before.

The hill is strangely community oriented. Such wildflowers as the brilliant blue lupine, scarlet paint-brush and orange globe mallow grow happily right in the lap of the prickly pear cactus. The lovely pink bitterroot, however, blooms on a rocky slope in an isolated area unappreciated by others.

On our way back, Ned stopped the car at the end of a culvert in a draw and turned off the motor.

"There's a little red nose sticking out of the culvert," he whispered.

I handed him the camera, cocked and ready to shoot.

"It's a baby fox," he murmured, trying to hold his hands steady as he aimed for action.

The kit was curious. Slowly, he crept toward us until he stood no more than four feet from our car. He sniffed and lifted his head as we shared a reciprocal star-ing. Ned snapped the camera over and over, talking to the kit in soft, gentle tones all the while.

Just as the film reached its end, the little fox reached the end of his curiosity, patience, or both, turned and disappeared from sight in the culvert. Maybe his mother called him to supper. We drove home to ours.

Like the bard said, "What is so rare as a day in June? Then, if ever, come perfect days."

This June, this day, brought us one of the best.

Grizzly bears are showing up in areas where none have been seen for years.

Ranger file photo

ANDY MEETS GRIZZLY

When you get to the end of your rope, tie a knot and hang on!
- Leo Buscaglia

"Go! Go! Go!" Andy yelled to his friend Dave in the pickup truck as Andy plunged head-first into the truck box with a grizzly hot on his heels.

Earlier that day, Andy talked of fishing up Burroughs Creek above Dubois.

"Did you see the signs warning that this is grizzly country?" asked Dave.

"Yeah, but I'm not going far," Andy replied. "Might be a beaver pond or two up there."

Dave, dealing with a backache that day, fished back toward the pickup while Andy walked on up 100 yards or so into a rough, more heavily forested area. Time passed. Since his luck hadn't pick up much, Andy headed back toward the pickup, stopping by the creek to decide if he'd clean his short catch now or later.

For no reason in particular Andy turned and looked behind him. He gasped. His heart leaped and began to pound. There, just a few yards away stood a grizzly bear, head down, digging busily in the soft black soil for grubs.

Andy froze. The silver tips of the charcoal-colored grizzly's coat flashed like a warning beacon in the noon-day sun. So far, the bear hadn't seen him.

Quickly, Andy took mental inventory. No gun. No bear spray. No weapon of any kind.

"If it's a sow with cubs," he thought, "My chances are better if she doesn't feel threatened."

With carefully chosen footsteps Andy began to move away, leaving his fishing pole behind.

Nearby Burroughs Creek sang her rippling song. Maybe, he thought, the sound would help conceal the crackle and crunch of twigs and leaves as he walked.

About 50 feet down the trail, despite the fact that his hair stood on end and chills chased each other up and down his spine, Andy couldn't resist looking back.

The bear stood, staring. Their eyes locked.

Andy turned quickly and proceeded about 40 yards toward the safety of the pickup. In his hurry, he tripped on a rock and fell.

"Dumb stunt!" he mumbled. Quickly, he caught himself and regained his foothold. How much time had he lost with one careless step?

Again, he glanced back. He must be nearly out of sight of the bear now, he thought, almost 2/3 of the way back to the pickup. He turned to make sure.

The grizzly came galloping toward him in great powerful bounds.

Andy burst ahead, running for his life as hard and fast as he could go. He cleared a dirt bank where the Forest Service had closed off an old logging road, thinking he'd almost escaped when a sinking thought hit him.

"What if Dave isn't back in the pickup? I'll be leading the bear to him. With his bad back he won't have a chance..."

But right now it was Andy the bear was after. That left no choice but to keep running as fast as he could.

Rounding the last corner of what seemed forever, Andy saw Dave's head in the pickup window and yelled, "Bear! Bear!"

Only about 15 feet remained now until the grizzly would close the gap between them. Andy knew he couldn't reach the passenger door, much less open it.

Vaulting into the pickup box Andy yelled, "Go! Go! Go!"

The grizzly rose to its hind legs, both paws over the tailgate with claws extended.

While Andy stared into the grizzly's face, petrified, Dave jammed his gears into reverse knocking the bear backward, stunned and confused.

Full speed ahead now, with Andy rattling around between tool boxes, coolers and fishing gear in the pickup box, Dave drove down the road a quarter of a mile or so and stopped. Andy crawled into the cab beside him, breathless and bruised, but probably the luckiest fisherman in Wyoming that day. Certainly, the one with the biggest story to tell.

Andy decided not to fish anymore that afternoon. He didn't have a pole, anyway.

Today, Dave has his own tale of what he saw in his rear view mirror, with bear claw scratches on his red pickup to support almost any version.

Andy's story is somewhat varied from the original. Distances are not as they seemed, he says, and when he measured it later he found the bear covered 300 yards faster even than Andy remembered. Having a grizzly on your tail can seem forever.

Andy's father, Herb, a lifelong explorer and writer on the Wyoming high country experience, taught his son many things.

"But that day," Andy says, "I broke many of the rules."

A very important one was failing to drop the creel that hung on his shoulder and may even have lured the bear his way.

"Looking into a grizzly's eyes," Andy declares, "Can do that to a man."

SKUNKED BY A SKUNK

How a person masters his fate is more important than what his fate is.   *- Wilhelm von Humboldt*

We've been chasing elusive black and white creatures around Pheasant Crest all fall. They're almost handsome in appearance. And I'd be willing to share my territory if they'd take a more subtle attitude toward life.

My first memory of the malodorous little animals called skunks is of my mother surprising one in the cornfield when I was a child. Mother was surprised too.

In those days one didn't part with clothing easily. Times were hard and fervent salvage efforts required. Mother buried her dress, stockings and shoes in the ground, waiting for nature to perform some sort of miracle. It didn't happen. Next, she soaked them in tomato juice, a drastic use of food in a growing family.

Other methods failed as well. Finally, she muttered, "Miserable wretch!" in the general direction of the cornfield and burned the offensive garments. When a creature was reduced to the state of "miserable wretch," you knew Mother's incredible patience was spent.

My own view of the little stinkers mellowed when our son at age six requested a skunk costume for a school Halloween party. Eventually, I created a fairly accurate version. Then he decided it would enhance his costume if he ran around at the party squirting perfume from an atomizer. Sure enough, at evening's end in a reeking gym he was awarded first prize. I suspect the judges' decision was born of a need to end the event and start breathing.

Our dog Tippi experienced a similar problem. One night he pursued a skunk until he caught it – on the end of his nose, clinging tightly with all four feet. Tippi raced toward the house howling for help.

Ned grabbed a shovel and ran to the dog's aid, hoping to dislodge the skunk. In the darkness, he missed. Then, discretion being the better part of valor as they say,

Ned made an abrupt decision to exit the scene.

Desperate, Tippi followed Ned to the house and gave one last vigorous shake. The skunk lost its hold and rolled across the porch, hitting the screen door full force just seconds after Ned ducked inside, yanking the door shut behind him. The skunk dropped from sight through a loose board in the porch.

Guess who won that round? Shuddering at how close we'd come to have a pungent ball of skunk roll into our living room, we moved over to stay with parents a few weeks while the odor dissipated.

The next encounter found Ned away from home, so I phoned his older brother widely known as "Tuffy."

Tuffy appeared, loaded his gun and waited. Shortly, the skunk walked out of the weeds along a ditch bank. Tuffy took aim. Just as he was about to fire, three darling baby skunks emerged from the weeds to fall in line single file behind their mother.

Tuffy's face crumpled. The gun dropped to his side. The man totally deserted his name.

"Aw hell, Betty…" was all he could say as he headed for his truck.

These little animals are as bold as their distinctive coloring. And that's considerably bolder than I am. One ambled up to our back step recently and handily held me at bay while he polished off the cat's food I'd just set out.

I was left with the option of waiting outside in the dark chilly night until he finished his banquet or beating on the windows to rouse Ned from a nap to let me in the locked front door. I chose the latter.

Someday, we're going to outwit one of the feisty beasts. But you'd better not wait for the story. The verb definition of "skunk" in the dictionary is "defeat."

BIRD BRAINS

Man is harder than iron, stronger than stone and more fragile than a rose.   *- Turkish proverb*

The father of my son has been learning about the birds and the bees recently, especially the birds. A bit late, you suspect? Read on.

A week or so ago, a robin decided to build her nest in one of the flower baskets my agronomist mate hung across the back of our breezeway inside the sliding glass doors. He considered it a very impractical spot for a nest, as the plants must be watered daily. And since there were no eggs there when he discovered it, he removed the nest hoping the bird might select a more sensible place like a tree.

But who says a robin is sensible? She has a bird brain, doesn't she?

Next morning, I stood on a chair and peeked into the basket. "There's a beautiful blue robin egg here in the mud," I announced.

Meantime, the garbage man came and hauled away the garbage, bird nest and all. Ned grabbed a handful of fresh green grass clippings and shaped them into what looked like a nest to him. He carefully placed the egg in it.

The robin returned, reshaped the nest, and laid another egg. Each morning now, while she goes off to find a worm or two and drink from the bird bath, Ned gingerly pours enough water into the side of the basket to try to keep his plant alive.

Rebuilding the nest was only the beginning.

We have to cross the breezeway to get from the house to the garage. Though several yards from her nest, mother robin considers this trespassing. She flies from the nest each time we go out what we thought was our own back door, watching warily from the wooden fence until we come back in or drive away in the car. Each day we grow less certain who owns this territory.

Now I'm beginning to feel guilty, myself. Why do we go in and out the back door so many times each day anyway?

"Maybe we could use the front door," I suggested. We tried that a few times, but it's quite a distance around the house and out to the garden via the detour that pleases our resident robin. It's also a darn nuisance. Wouldn't you think that bird could make a few adjustments herself if she's so determined to practice communal living? This arrangement, after all, was her idea.

She does seem to be adapting in some ways. Ned is outside in the yard and garden much more than I and I think she's gained a bit of trust in him. She stays on the nest more when he goes out. Then I remember - he helped rebuild her nest. And he cares for her landscaping and keeps her private swamp cooler functional. Maybe she's not so dumb.

A friend warns us, "You ain't seen nothin' yet."

"Just wait till her chicks hatch," she says. "She'll scold you and dive at you and drive you right out of here. She'll take over your yard, feed her children on your ripe strawberries and those fat fishing worms you stashed in the garden. Just wait."

This morning, we relayed our story to a neighbor with whom we walked the hiking trail. I told her about Ned rebuilding the robin's nest.

"What a nice man," she said.

And I thought of the man's son. "He won't kill a bug in the house," I told her. "He picks them up and helps them outside into their own environment."

Meanwhile, our daughter-in-law and I share our homes, along with a couple of nice men, with birds and others of nature's realm.

And I wonder anew about bird brains, when a robin in a flower pot can train two humans to her ways so quickly. Ah well, we're still learning about the birds and the bees.

ENTANGLED IN NATURE'S PLAN

In the right light, at the right time, everything is extraordinary.
- Aaron Rose

This might be called the second installment of a story for the birds. A few weeks ago, we found a robin nesting in a hanging flower basket in our breezeway. It occurs to me that a robin family's story may be as important in its way as Day in The Park, the Hot Air Balloon Rally, or our July wedding anniversary. Here's the conclusion. (I think.)

Three naked robin chicks emerged from the sky blue eggs. Their parents dutifully carried worms to them amid Ned's and my comings and goings and occasional peeks into their nest. We watched the chicks slowly clothe themselves in white fuzz and finally, feathers. By now, we were a familiar part of their environment.

The family picnic we'd planned for our breezeway on July 4 was quite a different matter.

"I can't imagine the parents will fly in here among a crowd of eating, laughing, story-telling people," I worried. "Not even to feed their young."

The robin chicks were growing fast. But could they possibly leave the nest by picnic day?

Then a neighbor told us of baby birds he'd seen fall onto a concrete floor to their death.

"I'll put a big hook on the eave just outside the glass breezeway doors and hang their basket nest out there," Ned decided. "Then they can land in a flower garden."

No sooner had he made the move when a rain and wind storm blew in. The basket swung wildly in the wind and rain poured down on the baby birds.

"They're so young. They'll get pneumonia." Ned brought the flower basket, birds and all, back inside the breezeway and hung it on its original hook. Mama and Papa Robin appeared a bit puzzled but continued to feed the family while their nest moved mysteriously (to them) from inside the breezeway to the outside several more times as weather dictated.

After a week or so, the baby robins were adapting well to the out-of-doors. Now, when the wind blew an afternoon gale from the west, the young birds lifted their heads, turned their beaks to the wind and leaned into it as if it were merely a fresh breeze.

July 4 arrived. Humans filled the breezeway. If the robins had found Ned and I an intrusion, they must have felt this a major test. Yet even with 16 eating, laughing, chatting humans just the other side of the glass doors, the birds were not daunted. They continued to stuff their young with worms with even more zeal than before. We did something quite similar ourselves, though I thought our food a better choice.

Later, the crowd carried their chairs to the big attached garage to sing to the music of the Lowrey organ stored there, its tunes coaxed forth by a brother who still can't decide if he's a musician or comedian. Unfazed by our noise and nonsense, the robins continued to feed their chicks. Between worms, the chicks stretched their wings and preened their feathers.

Next day, we carried our morning mugs of coffee to the breezeway. To our surprise, two baby robins were already gone from the nest. The smallest of the trio, the one with lingering tufts of white fuzz pushing up through the feathers on his head, perched on the edge of the basket peering down toward the ground. You could almost envision him wailing in disbelief, "You mean 'way down there? I'm supposed to jump out of this nest into that big strange world?"

Mother Robin perched on the nearby wooden fence, her short chirps urging in bird language, "Come! Come! Come!"

Baby looked warily to the ground time and again, teetering on the edge of the basket-nest, then backing down into it. Finally, she brought him a long worm, allowed only a taste, then pulled it away and flew back to the fence to cluck some more, "Come! Come!"

Suddenly, the small chick with little white tufts waving atop his head climbed to the edge of his hanging basket home and toppled to the flower garden. He bounced off the wooden fence one time, a bit dazed. Back on his feet, he looked about, took a few steps, then hopped out to the vegetable garden. He seemed to know there was protection beneath the raspberry bushes, fish worms to eat, and perhaps an occasionally strawberry for dessert.

And the humans in this story? Did we ever question our involvement in nature's plan? Yes, regularly. But whose idea was it for us to live in the bird world anyway?

PART V

HISTORY

Peering into The Past -

These stories explore but a few of the events and places that built Wyoming's rich past, often affecting the entire country while lending the state's people the character and color that defines them today.

Original trail to Hole-in-The-Wall, still used today by automobiles.

Author's photo

Sunlight leaks through the clouds with rare timing to highlight historic Hole-in-The Wall (center of photo) where The Wild Bunch hid out in the late 1800s.

Author's photo

HOLE-IN-THE-WALL

The average man will bristle if you say his father was dishonest, but he will brag a little if he discovers that his great-grandfather was a pirate.   *- Bern Williams*

Why are people so obsessed with the times and trails of the outlaws? I've asked the question of a number of people, including myself more than once. No one responds with the quick, bursting light bulb answer I'd hoped for. Yet unless you were there, you wouldn't believe the crowd that joined a trek to Hole-in-the-Wall where The Wild Bunch hid out in the late 1800s.

Today, that notorious spot is part of the Willow Creek Ranch owned by Gene and Sammye Veigh and may be explored only by invitation. On a bright spring day, Worland, Wyoming guide Clay Gibbons, expecting maybe eight or ten 4-wheel drive vehicles for the rugged trek, finds himself leading a procession of at least 65. Vehicles, that is. Most are loaded with passengers.

The route takes us through miles and miles of beautiful red and green hills dotted with black Angus cattle. At the base of Rough-lock Hill, we walk through a carpet of pink, purple, yellow and white wildflowers while Clay tells of early ranchers whose closest access to the valley was over the steep hill behind us. Here, tree branches or sticks of wood were placed between spokes of wagon wheels with the idea that a slow skid would be better than a fast roll. This was the "rough lock" for which the hill is named.

We travel on past red rock bluffs standing like dominoes, 18 or 20 in a row. Each rusty projection looks almost identical to the other, pushing up toward white sailboat clouds in a bright blue sky.

Now we're on dirt road and a fine red dust rises up and envelops our vehicles. We turn on our headlights to avoid running over each other.

This is the very road traveled on horseback by Butch Cassidy, the Sundance Kid, the James Brothers, Tom Horn, Tom Oday, Kid Curry and others more than 100 years ago. With the red clouds boiling around us, ghosts of history emerge from a time warp of our minds.

"What will Butch and Sundance think if they see all this dust coming at them across the valley?" Ned asks.

"Probably that we're the biggest and scariest posse ever," I guess. "Maybe the U.S. Cavalry."

With the sun nearly eclipsed and the road blurred by clouds of red dust, I drift further into twists of time. "Maybe the outlaw trail has collided with the dust bowl," I suggest.

By now, it's taking all my mate's attention to find the road. Reality has returned. I get only a wry smile for response.

It wouldn't be much fun to go on a trek without your mind tuned to the past, though. In this case, to the 25-30 years this valley was ruled by outlaws who befriended ranchers of the area and robbed from those in neighboring states. Here, the stolen cattle were fattened on the abundant natural grassland and rebranded for illegal sale. Brands were sometimes cut out and the animals' hide stitched back together. With a little regrowth of hair a new brand could be cleverly created. Suddenly, I see in the outlaws the original cosmetic surgeons.

At Hole-in-the-Wall monument, Clay, a tall, slim cowboy type wearing a black hat and an easy smile, draws his six-shooter from its holster and fires a shot in the air. Old west history comes alive as Clay relates the story of the Hole-in-the-Wall fight near this spot on July 22, 1897.

Here, gutsy Bob Divine of CY Cattle Company and 11 others engaged in a fiery gun battle with several members of the Hole-in-the-Wall gang. Despite death and injury to some, Divine and his men returned shortly after to retrieve hundreds of stolen cattle from the outlaws. "Where were the sheriffs and their posses?" one trekker asks. "Why was all this allowed?"

"Two main reasons," Clay explains. "The extremely difficult access to the area and fear of the Wild Bunch who lived and died by their own rules. They shot or hung each other if their law decreed it."

We picnic near Buffalo Creek just a few yards below where Hole-in-the-Wall cabin once stood. Only the foundation remains, this day surrounded by tents occupied by a group of visitors from Italy who question our intrusion. Clay assures them he has the ranchers' permission to lead us there.

"But did they know there'd be this many vehicles?" one asks.

"Doubt it," says Clay. "Didn't know myself 'til this morning."

After lunch, we continue driving over a winding, steep and treacherous trail that breaks the front axle of one trekker's 4-wheel-drive pickup. We're a sobered bunch.

When we get to Hole-in-the-Wall, the view is awesome, colorful and seemingly endless. Perhaps the most surprising geographic fact is that there's no mysterious cave or cavern as many envision, but a steep broken trail of rubble leading up to a red rock mesa with a magnificent overlook of the valleys below. The hole itself is accessible only by horseback, the area of penetration from any direction so small that two sharpshooters could hold off an entire army.

So did this dramatic trip into the past tell me why law-abiding people are obsessed with outlaw history? I still don't have a clue. But if a prize were to be awarded for the best answer, I think I'd hand it to the smiling man who offered, "Maybe there's a little outlaw in all of us."

YELLOWSTONE PARK FIRES

What I'm looking for is a blessing that's not in disguise.
- Kitty O'Neill Collins

A man in Oklahoma once told me, "Those Wyoming mountains scare me to death! I'd never go back."

"Why?" I asked.

"Because," he said, "I looked down and the gorges and canyons below were endless. I was so frightened I could hardly drive."

"You should have been scared," I replied. "Why weren't you watching the road?"

I thought it humorous, but he didn't laugh.

I'm not fearful of driving up there. But I must admit the Yellowstone forest fires gave me spooky feelings that summer of 1988.

For weeks we watched the Owl Creek, Absaroka and Wind River Mountain ranges move in and out of a smoky shroud. Every time I rejoiced that the great blue peaks were emerging, they retreated again. The forest fires seemed endless. It was sad, and in a way, quite eerie.

Some mornings we awoke in confusion.

"Where's the sun?" I asked.

"Clock must be wrong," Ned answered.

About a half-hour late, the sun rose above the smoke on the horizon, then shone weakly through an orange-gray haze, much like an eclipse. The effects of the fires were felt by human, animal and plant life alike.

Some residents had to take children out of the area to recover from health problems caused by the smoke. Herds of bighorn mountain sheep and deer descended to farms and ranches near Dubois in search of safety, feed and water. And plant life? Debatable, apparently. The Forest Service said, "Let it burn. It's a natural thing." But I and many others were sad so much beauty was turning to ashes.

Adding to the strange atmosphere at our country home was a mysterious nocturnal bird who announced his presence with a weird, raucous squawk at regular intervals just as we dropped off to sleep. Perhaps he had a sore throat from the smoke.

I, nearly always upbeat and optimistic, began showing signs of discouragement at being hemmed in by the heavy smoke. Some days, the feeling was one of near fright; other times, just sorrow. Home, to me, is surrounded by beautiful mountains and their mystery and magic. Now I felt estranged, kicked out.

This alien environment led me to introspection. What is it about these leaping projections of earth that so enchants us; pulls at us when we're away; insists we return, no matter how far we wander?

Some might say, "fishing," some, "hunting," some, "hiking." Of course it's all these. But it's more.

I wonder if it's that our Creator makes his presence so obvious in the mountains, the vastness of his work putting us and our self-importance in humbling perspective. It prepares us for renewal. Up there, the silence makes us listen to its message. We can't argue with it. We don't even want to. We just want to forget the sometimes irrational world down below and say, "More. Tell me more."

American religious writer and poet, Thomas Merton, observed, "It's hard to be neurotic in front of a bunch of trees."

That's one thing you can affirm up there. Another is, it's hard to deny who's really in charge of this Earth.

One week, an ominous looking storm blew in. Skies darkened with varying strange colors, and a huge unidentified rolling object crossed the western horizon. Cars on the highway sped for cover and some people headed for underground protection.

We'd been attacked by nothing more than another gigantic belch of smoke!

Each day, we looked forward to the day we could see the mountains from this valley again and feel the clarity of their call to us, be it spiritual, recreational, or simply a sense of oneness with our environment.

Day after day, week after week, we waited. . . . .

THE DAY THE FIRES DROWNED

Life is uncharted territory. It reveals its story one moment at a time.
                                                    - Leo Buscaglia

Once out of bed and upright, I love driving early in the morning. It lends itself to unusual encounters. But how early is early?

Ned and I planned a trip to the mountains to cut firewood in one of the few areas where the Forest Service allowed such activity with much of Yellowstone Park still burning or in danger that summer of 1988. We wanted to make a one-day trip, but woodcutting was only allowed from 6 a.m. until noon.

The alarm rang. It was 3:30 A.M.

"I thought we were going to leave at 4:00," I moaned, pulling the pillow over my head.

"Right. Get up at 3:30, leave at 4:00," Ned clipped, feet already on the floor.

By a little before 6:00, we were in a cafe in Dubois pleading for coffee. The young waitress seemed dismayed that people our age were out at that hour. Frankly, I was a little dismayed myself. Then I remembered the advice of humorist Ashleigh Brilliant, "The older you get, the more important it is not to act your age." That means get your head off the table.

"You came all the way from Riverton to cut wood?" the waitress asked in amazement.

"Yeah. This is where the wood is."

We weren't sure what we should have been doing, but I don't suppose she did see many people "our age" who'd risen at 3:30 a.m. to cut wood in the mountains. It wasn't as if we'd freeze to death next winter if we didn't do it.

"Are you a logger?" She eyed Ned curiously. That would, I suppose, make us more credible.

"No. I just like the woods." (He also had a new chainsaw.)

"Then maybe you should have been a logger," she suggested.

I wondered if she really thought he'd missed his calling, or if she was stalling for time until she had a chance to phone "the home" and tell them we'd escaped. She fed us and let us go.

As we drove, we saw two ratty-coated coyotes rambling along the road not seeming to fear us at all.

"Maybe highway vehicles don't look so threatening when compared to forest fires," Ned observed.

On the mountain, with a spark arrester on our chainsaw, 10 gallons of water and a fire extinguisher aboard to comply with that year's forest regulations, we began to fill our pickup and horse trailer with wood.

In the small draw where we worked, smoke from the forest fires hung dense and oppressive, invading my sinuses and all the dips and hollows of the land. The sun rose blood red as if suffering its own kind of pain.

By 11 o'clock, the skies began to change color. Between us and a distant blue shadow mountain hung a white curtain. The air grew chilly. Suddenly, I saw a tiny snowflake drifting down in front of me - a beautiful blessed snowflake! Never had we been so happy to see the first sign of winter in September.

All the way back to Dubois and below, we watched the great crystals fall in torrents, turning the ground soft, white and gloriously wet. Our spirits took wings. Maybe the snow would douse the Yellowstone inferno!

Down home in the valley, it was only a cloudy day, one that in other times might be considered dreary and depressing. Today, the pearly gray clouds looked gorgeous. Clouds instead of smoke. Truly a day for unusual things!

I inhaled the fresh smelling air, dreaming of the rugged dark blue horizons that might soon emerge. In imagination, I danced down the street barefoot, stopped on the corners to toss flowers to passersby and balloons to the skies.

Filled with a freedom of spirit I hadn't known for some time, I called out to nearly everyone I met, "If you want to kick loose and let your heart be merry, just go ahead." Then, with true feelings unleashed, I added, "And if your behavior brings in someone with a butterfly net, tell him to go fill it with smoke!"

NEW LIFE PARK

One of the wonders of life is just that - the wonder of life.
- Bill Copeland

A year after the devastating 1988 forest fires, Ned and I drove up to Yellowstone Park to see what had happened. Sitting speechless in the car seat beside one another, we swallowed our tears. We didn't take any pictures. Now I wish I had, but at the time it seemed a little like taking pictures of a casket when a loved one dies.

Four years after the fires, we snowmobiled through the park in January. The wintertime view made the area seem even more a graveyard. Blackened trees stood dark against the snow, casting long, haunting reflections of death.

We still didn't take pictures of the destruction.

In 1998, a decade after the burn, I shot up film as if it grew on fireweed, eager to record the exciting and uplifting education on Earth's ability to heal herself. Park Service and Forest Service officials were pleased. But they too learned that powerful elements of nature can't always be controlled by man.

In most burn locations the forest still stood, barren and charred posts looming against a clear blue sky. In areas where the soil was shallow or hard winds blew, many of the ghostly trees had fallen.

Regrowth, where the fire was most intense and the earth itself was seared, grew sparse and slow. Elsewhere, lush new life carpeted the forest floor. A type of bunch-grass was prevalent in most areas, glowing with fields of beautiful lavender-pink fireweed. In places, purple mountain asters and white yarrow and yampah were sprinkled among them. In other areas, small yellow flowers added warmth and eye-catching light to the scene.

Young pines poked their fresh greenness up from the scorched earth, a vivid contrast to their cremated parents still standing guard and offering, perhaps, a measure of protection. After a decade, most young trees grew only 2 to 3 feet tall. A few stood as high as 5 or 6 feet. An occasional baby aspen danced in the mountain breeze.

No animals were seen that day in such areas. The new growth offered no camouflage and perhaps not yet the type forage they like. Trees were too small to offer protection for birds, so none were sighted here. Only a few insects such as a bumblebee and a butterfly find such locations habitable in this stage of regrowth.

Just two years later, in the year 2000, we saw a young deer in the same area, seeming to feel quite at home. Already, the trees are taller, undergrowth much more dense and forage varied and plentiful.

Young deer greets visitors to Yellowstone's new growth area.

Author's photo

Grizzled bison nibbles new bunch grass in Yellowstone burn area.
Author's photo

Amid barren trees charred by 1988 fires, lush new life–including lavender-pink fireweed, purple mountain asters, and white yarrow and yampah–carpets the forest floor in Yellowstone National Park.
Author's photo

Tourists drove through constantly. Park Service and Forest Service officials hoped they'd stop to observe the awesome display of life recreating itself. Few travelers slowed or got out to walk through this great drama of violent death and rebirth in action.

Perhaps people expected it to happen faster. One of the great lessons man might learn from the Yellowstone fires is that nature is much more patient than he, that her measure is eons, not years. But then, as one viewer wryly observed, "Nature has more time."

Devils Tower

Author's photo

DEVILS TOWER: HISTORY AND MYSTERY

As far as trails go, there's always an open trail for the mind if you keep the doors open and give it a chance.

- Louis L'Amour

The first mystery is dispelled when you discover this massive column of stone does not belong to the devil. Its name is Devils Tower, not the possessive, Devil's Tower. Through clerical error when it was designated the first national monument of the United States by President Theodore Roosevelt in 1906, an apostrophe was eliminated. The rest of its mysteries live and grow along with the imaginations of humans who visit there.

The very sight of the tower speaks to the senses, no matter what one's interest in the nearly 1300 foot lava projection. Maybe it's the way the huge mass of vertical columns moves mysteriously in and out of sight as you approach, now hiding behind the mist, now shining in the sun like a great petrified tree stump rising from its forested base.

Maybe it's the spiritual aspect revered by American Indians since the 1700s, and the legends it inspires. Or the challenge to climbers, to the parachutist who spent days atop the great rock awaiting rescue. Or aliens haunting the tower in Steven Spielberg's unforgettable movie, *Close Encounters of The Third Kind.*

A mile-long hike around the tower's base allows time to consider them all.

Called Bear Lodge, Bear's Lair, Bear's Tipi and other names by various tribes of early Indians, the tower shares its stories mostly through humans who invite them into their dreams. Since early Indians related to many life events symbolically, they often envisioned the long striations in the monument resulting from bear claws. One such legend tells of a boy who turns into a bear and chases young girls to the tower's top. Another version of the same story has young girls climbing a large rock to escape a bear. Since he could still reach them there, the Great Spirit raised the rock skyward to save the girls. The bear tried to jump to the top but could not. His claws scratched the deep marks into the rock as he fell.

Because of the tower's unique size and appearance, the Indian people viewed it then and now as majestic and holy in nature. Today, Devils Tower is reserved for sacred tribal events at designated periods of the year. Climbing is prohibited at such times.

Perhaps one of the most fascinating true stories of Devils Tower is that of 29-year-old daredevil George Hopkins' landing atop the great rock. On October 1, 1941, Hopkins jumped from a plane and parachuted 1200 feet to land safely despite a brisk wind. A skinned ankle was his only injury. But the story didn't end there.

Hopkins' plan was to stay an hour or two, then rappel down. When his pilot dropped climbing equipment and ropes for descent, they bounced off the rock and snagged on bushes about 50 feet down the side of the tower. The pilot returned to Rapid City, S. Dak. and could not be reached.

Veteran Spearfish pilot Clyde Ice flew in, dropped another rope which reached Hopkins so tangled it was useless. Ice returned, dropping blankets, tarpaulin and food to help the parachutist weather a cold night of rain and sleet.

Hopkins now decided he'd leap off the tower and parachute to the ground. That plan ended abruptly when Washington, D.C. Park Service officials nixed the idea. Instead, they sent for professional Colorado climbers to assist. Meantime, Clyde Ice, experienced in hospital mercy flights and flood and fire disasters, continued to drop life-sustaining supplies to Hopkins. To deal with strong tower updrafts, Ice cut his motor and flew about six feet above the tower's top, dropped the food and shelter items, then restarted his motor and flew on.

(This part of the pilot's derring-do particularly intrigues this author, since I remember my mother telling of Clyde Ice wanting her to ride in his plane with him when she was a young woman. She declined, she said, considering Ice "a bit reckless.")*

Ice continued to assist Hopkins until Wyoming's famed climber, Paul Petzoldt, drove in from Jackson Hole in a snowstorm to head a rescue team. In cold and treacherous weather, the climbers finally escorted Hopkins from his unplanned six day stay on the 1.5 acre tower top.

Thousands from around the world have felt challenged by the great monument, and many climb it. William Rogers and Willard Ripley made the first ascent on July 4, 1893, on a wooden ladder they built themselves. Rogers wife, Linnie, used the ladder to become the first woman to climb the tower. Parts of that structure remain fastened between the several-sided columns to this day, and can be seen with binoculars from the ground.

In 1976, the mysterious monument that seems to cast a spell over everyone just because it is there, caught the imagination of film director Steven Spielberg. Soon filming crews and hundreds of onlookers as well as a number of Wyoming residents flocked to the area to watch or become a part of the popular movie, *Close Encounters of The Third Kind.*

During the 12 days of filming on location at Devils Tower, helicopters pursued supposed outer space vehicles that hovered, pulsed with mysterious lights, and eventually lured a small boy aboard the huge saucer-shaped craft. The movie was a top money-maker. Scarcely anyone failed to see it, and to this day few have forgotten the haunting tale.

---

*When the "reckless," (or was it simply gutsy?) Clyde Ice applied for a Wyoming big game hunting license at age 100, his request was denied by the state. Then-Governor Mike Sullivan overruled the denial and Ice got his elk. He shot it himself.

The legends of Devils Tower continue to be told and retold, with new ones added as time goes on and the human spirit responds to the great rock's call. But contemporary Kiowa author N. Scott Momaday perhaps best explains reaction to the monument in his book, *The Way to Rainy Mountain*, with these words, "There are things in nature that engender an awful quiet in the heart of man; Devils Tower is one of them."

VIETNAM MEMORIAL

I look upon the whole world as my fatherland, and every war has to me the horror of a family feud.   *- Helen Keller*

Way out in Wyoming, it still calls to you. It still haunts you. It won't let you go.

The sheer simplicity of 58,219 names in stark white against the reflective black background of the Vietnam Veterans Memorial replica pulls like a magnet. You couldn't remain aloof if you tried.

In July, 1999, my mate of many years and I drove to Casper to celebrate our wedding anniversary in the city where we were married. We'd heard a traveling replica of the wall was on display in Fort Caspar Park and decided to stop on our way into town. It's impossible to anticipate the impact.

Called "The Wall that Heals," the replica is a half-scale model - exactly to the letter and inch - of the original Vietnam Veterans Memorial in Washington, D.C. Each of the two walls of the replica is approximately 123 feet long. The walls meet at an angle of 121 degrees and rise to a height of approximately 5 feet at their apex. The list of names begins at the apex with the first casualty and continues to the end of that wing. It resumes at the beginning of the opposite wing, ending at the apex.

Emotionally, the wall resists description. For each, it has its own message.

On this day, a hush hangs over the grassy park shaded by huge old trees. In the distance, a mourning dove issues its doleful call. We hesitate. Our hands connect and we're strengthened. We move slowly as we approach the long structure, humbled by this great gathering of heroes. They seem to speak for veterans of all wars who gave their lives for us. So many to whom we owe so much.

The strange quiet stills the four flags hanging nearby - Old Glory, Wyoming's state flag, The Vietnam Veterans, and the POW-MIA flags, the last one bearing the line, "You are not forgotten."

A huge cottonwood tree stands guard over Vietnam Veterans' Memorial replica as it visits Casper, Wyoming.

Author's photo

A near prayerful state comes over us. At the base of the monument are scattered wild flowers in simple vases and baskets, here and there a single red or pink rose, a poem, a touching letter or message. Some visitors caress the wall. Some do pencil rubbings to hold close to their hearts.

The list of names seems endless. With the eloquent voice of silence, they speak. The veil between us grows fragile, delicate and sheer. Time and space fade into bonded humanity. All become kin.

People walk quietly, almost speechless, sometimes whispering or murmuring low. There's a cough, a sniffle, a clearing of throats. My own swells with lumps of pain. I lower my sunglasses, fancying I can hide my tears. It doesn't work. My nose begins to run. The hastily grabbed white tissue waves my grief to everyone.

No one sees. They're busy dealing with their own.

I remember the shameful taunts and name-calling that once greeted returning Vietnam veterans, already struggling with feelings of conflict, nightmares of war and devastating physical injuries. Such cruel response from fellow countrymen still seems to me the greatest cowardice of all.

When we finally leave the wall, almost reluctantly now, we're struck with a painful irony. We come to Casper this day to celebrate many happy years of a life rich with blessings. These 58,219 young people scarcely got to begin theirs.

What do you say to such heroes? "Thank you," of course. "Thank you. . .Thank you, unending." Our souls stand naked in their presence. What will we do to prevent another war? To repay the thousands upon thousands who gave their lives for us through the years?

As a child, I learned a poem about Flanders Field, a soldiers' burial site in Belgium where my father fought in World War I, his own helmet bullet-creased. The poem, written by Canadian Col. Ray McRae in 1915, begins, "In Flanders Field the poppies blow, between the crosses row on row . . . . . We are the dead. Short days ago, we lived, felt dawn, saw sunset glow; loved and were loved, and now we lie - in Flanders Field."

As parts of the poem come to me, I watch the Vietnam Veterans Memorial turn into a haunting black and white Flanders Field. In words that speak to the ages, the poem ends, "If ye break faith with we who die, we shall not sleep though poppies grow, in Flanders field."

In poignant silence, they wait . . .

SOUTH PASS CITY

Presence is more than just being there.   *- Malcolm S. Forbes*

Curious and history-minded, Ned and I drove over to South Pass to learn more of our state's beginnings and experience that unique place from today's vantage point as well. The area, known as "the spine of America," is rich with history, told and untold.

South Pass City, which lies adjacent to the Oregon-California Trail, was born of the lure of gold. James Sherlock, who grew up in that wild and remote mountain town, writes in his book, *South Pass and Its Tales,* that bits of gold were first discovered in the area in the 1860s by a small detachment of soldiers sent from Ft. Bridger to find horse thieves, presumably the Hole-in-The Wall Gang who'd raided a Mormon settlement and stolen their horses.

When the chase was abandoned because of the large number of Indians in the area, the soldiers returned to Willow Creek, below the present site of South Pass City. There they noticed a few sparkles in the creek near their camp. Since many were mountain men and guides, they stayed on a bit to pan the alluring gravel in the stream.

Results were exciting; the price of gold at $18.75 per ounce even more so. The troops returned in the fall of 1866. The first gold was produced in what was later named Carissa Gulch. Thereafter, hills, streets and businesses about the area assumed the colorful name, along with the famous and richly endowed Carissa (Cariso) Mine.

On the north side of South Pass Avenue, the historic Carissa Saloon soon rose up and led a lively, raucous life. It still stands today, open to the public at designated times.

Ned and I spent most of our Independence Day visit in the old Carissa Saloon.

With that line, you might imagine us staggering out and being helped onto the shuttle bus for safe return to our car at the top of the hill. But that's not how it happened.

After a generous lunch up the street a way, costing only $3.50 and eaten in the ambience of mountain breezes wafting over cow chips, we wandered back to the Carissa Saloon. We'd been told a man named Henry Hudson would entertain there with his mandolin.

In the saloon where history expresses itself in aged decor, the smell of dust and old wood, we sat in chairs painted bawdy red, utterly charmed by Henry's rollicking oldtime music. A young couple from Green River, courageous or reckless enough to try dancing to tunes of their grandparents' youth, bounced about the floor.

Gradually, the music moved forward in time. And gradually, I found myself tapping my toes and humming along with more familiar songs. Suddenly, there was "Elmer's Tune!" I could hardly stay in my chair. In fact, if I'd dared, I could have danced on the bar.

Actually, I hoped Ned might spring to his feet and whirl me around the floor a few times. So what if we both wore sponge-soled shoes and the aging boards in the floor lay in careless conjoinment? Surely, "Elmer's Tune" could lift us above all these earthly obstacles!

But my mate isn't as impulsive as I. I couldn't get him to his feet to guide me over the bumps and barriers, and I didn't want to make a fool of myself. Not all alone, anyway.

Henry performed for at least an hour. People came and went, but we stayed. Many lingered to snap a picture of the man with the tapping feet and singing mandolin.

Still, Henry felt little glory. Directly behind him on the wall hung a huge old painting of a nude woman. He was sure every snap of the camera was only a sly attempt to photograph the reclining form on the blue sheet.

The figure in the painting, which I noticed was shaped a lot like the bass viol leaning against the wall below, caught the attention of all who entered the room.

One man covered another's eyes. A small boy pointed toward the woman, staring. His mother rolled her eyes away, shook her head and said, "Tsk, tsk," as any proper mother of Carissa's heyday would have done, had she entered the saloon at all.

When Henry left, we remained in our chairs to drift deeper into history as Lynn Swanson of Cheyenne entered, wearing a long green calico dress and black shawl. Lynn would portray, in an hour long monologue, Mary Walker, the first white mother to cross the Rockies with children.

Adeptly, Lynn led us back to the years of 1840-43. Soon, we knew Mary and her family well. Suddenly she leaned forward, looked deep into my eyes and said with great passion, "And thank you so much, Mrs. Perkins, for lending your *Pilgrim's Progress* book to my Isabella. She so yearns for something to read!"

I couldn't keep the tears from my eyes. Recalling how I'd hungered for and treasured the books of my own childhood, I knew I must, for that moment, indeed be Mrs. Perkins.

After several enchanting hours in the Carissa Saloon, believe it or not we went looking for a drink. But by now the delicious homemade lemonade at the stand next door was all gone.

"Here, have some fresh well water," said an old-fashioned looking lady, handing us each a modern-day paper cup. A man at the hand-powered pump nearby filled the cups with cool, refreshing water and we drank with all the appreciation of dusty-throated gold miners.

I couldn't help thinking what irony time had wrought. Here we'd spent most of an afternoon in the famous Carissa Saloon and had to go elsewhere for a drink! I ran back into the saloon and looked up at the nude woman in the painting who'd watched it all happen. Surely she'd turn over on her sheet at this travesty of time.

But no. She just lay there smiling her Mona Lisa smile, apparently satisfied with the modern world. Or maybe she was simply smirking at how she'd stolen the show today from Henry Hudson, with no effort at all.

At home that evening, we realized that stepping back through a window in time makes one hunger for more of its secrets. I returned to Sherlock's book to learn that the U.S. Mint credits the Carissa Mine with production of nearly a million dollars worth of gold. Other records place it closer to two or three million, a good deal of wealth in those days.

Low grade ore in considerable amounts remains to this day in the area, but present mining costs make the venture prohibitive. Now, summer visitors from near and far come to learn the history of South Pass and enjoy the thrill of panning out a few tiny nuggets of gold.

South Pass City is also the home of one particular being of all-time importance to women of America and maybe of the world. Esther Hobart Morris, who was born in 1814 and died in 1902, became the first woman justice of the peace in the U.S. She probably carries the world record for that achievement, as well. Morris was also a longtime proponent of women's right to vote.

The site of her home is at the east end of South Pass Avenue on the south side of the street. An archeological dig was done at the site in 1995-96, in hope of finding objects and artifacts that might reveal more of that historic place and time. Except for a few small items, the dig confirmed only that this was indeed the Morris home-site, agreeing with Esther's drawing

The right to vote was first granted this nation's women in 1869. It happened at Wyoming's first territorial assembly in Cheyenne, when members of the Council and House of Representatives granted that controversial right and earned Wyoming the name it still carries today, "The Equality State."

THE DESERT REGISTER

What lies behind us and what lies before us are small matters compared to what lies within us.   - Ralph Waldo Emerson

Independence Rock speaks. It can work a time warp on your mind.

As we stop and step out of our car beside the historic rock, a large troupe of young people in costume pass on foot with handcarts, re-enacting the emigrant experience of the Mormon/Oregon trail.

"Come on, climb to the top with me," urges my mate, grabbing my hand and pulling me toward the famous rock.

At the base of the "Desert Register" as the emigrants of the 1800s dubbed it, winds a narrow path. Here, wild roses fill the breeze with their fragrance. Bright yellow potentilla blossoms and sometimes another pink rose light the dark crevices as we climb. How can these lovely flowers thrive in the wee bit of soil that has blown into the wrinkles of rock? Is shelter sometimes more vital to life than food?

The breathtaking climb stimulates thought as well as circulation. Why do humans still cling to this great granite outcropping, struggle to its top to find the smooth, rosy-beige spaces that invite them to carve their names and dates of visit?

Is their need akin to the flowers that strive to root and shout with bright bloom their existence in this forbidding environment? Do we and they, like the early emigrants, turn to a body more lasting than ours to speak to the ages of our presence here?

I imagine the huge, immutable promontory exerting some kind of magnetic force, pulling at man and plant, the colorful mobile creatures, with the message, "Come. Be a part of me."

Independence Rock silently speaks names and dates of long ago emigrants, while modern day Mormons re-enact the famous westward movement.

Author's photo

The wild rose and potentilla seeds riding the whims of the wind land where the breeze drops them and lend colorful life to the boulder. But man, the one with his own logic, responds to the rock, "You exist here through the ages. I, generally less than a century. I'll join you any way I can."

At the summit, as below, we find names and dates everywhere, ranging from the 1840s to the 1920s and on up to more recent years. The need for humans to leave a sign of themselves and their passing as a part of something more lasting is evident.

A man bearing the name of my husband's maternal ancestors traversed the area for seven years, each date marked beside his name. Clearly, he was an adventurer. I begin to see the importance of my following his descendant to meet today's challenge. What kind of emigrant wife am I, anyway?

When we finally work our way down to the rock's base, we come to more wild roses snuggled into a familied circle of soft-leafed sage. Nearby, lupine flashes its royal blue from the tall grass. Here and there at the foot of the Desert Register we come upon a delicate pink bitterroot shyly hugging the earth.

Were all these lovely flowers here when the emigrants crossed? I hope so. With the endless illness and hardship they endured, they'd have needed all they could find of nature's bright food for the soul.

A short distance from the rock we read the wry observation of Jesuit Missionary Pierre Jean DeSmet: "Some of the names left here perhaps ought not to be found anywhere." Could be. Yet the great rock accepts and preserves them all.

We turn and step into our modern day prairie schooner with bathroom, refrigerator and cookstove. The strange time warp releases its hold, and so does the magnetic rock. We climbed it. Our visit is recorded only in photographs and memory.

* * * * * * * * * *

At home, the time warp awakens, embraces me. I read and re-read the journals of those brave travelers of the trail. And like a wildflower seed fallen into the wrinkles of rock, I take root and become a part of that awesome era that built our world today.

INDEPENDENCE ROCK - 1843

We found a passel of emigrants here,
at the desert register,
either in person or name.
Passed Sweetwater, yesterday, where
bleak and naked granite rocks, like
craggy heads look down
on alkali lagoons . . .
The Rockies, sure, are aptly
called - rocks piled on rocks,
magnificent and strange in shape.
Our oxen teams are wearied -
hungry, lame, and near give out.
Supplies grow lean. The cholera's bad;
graves line the trail; like scouts,
they mark our way. The Indians came -
they only took two cows; we thank
the Lord. Drove off a pack of wolves
last night. Layed by today, to gather
chips, to wash, make bread.
Dried buffalo, as hard as wood,
cooked long enough, makes soup. And though
tomorrow's grim, tonight, along the trail
to Oregon, the fiddles play,
our people dance - It's
Independence Day!

–Betty Starks Case

A trekker returns from a long, reflective hike on the famous Oregon Trail.

Author's photo

Protected from wolf and coyote predation by piles of rock, many emigrant graves line the Oregon Trail.

Author's photo

TREKKING THE TRAIL

You can't test courage cautiously.   *- Annie Dillard*

To better sense its history, my mate and I decide to walk a portion of the shadowy Oregon Trail. A move through windows to the past demands solitude. On Wyoming's old South Pass, we head in opposite directions that each might seek our own response.

Meandering across miles and miles of hills and valleys, the trail looks much as it probably did in 1843, except that the wagon tracks have dimmed. This year the prairies are so lush from spring rains, a band of sheep almost loses itself in the tall new growth. Sagebrush cleansed by morning dew smells spicy and fresh among scattered wild onions, an occasional pink bitterroot and patches of orange globe mallow. The fragrance and color awaken the senses. The past seems to seep through the soles of my heavy hiking boots as I walk.

I think of the women pioneers who expected they might be riding more than walking. As oxen tired or died and wagon parts wore out, women and children often found themselves on this rocky trail with clumsy, makeshift footwear that soon wore to shreds. Raw and bleeding feet were wrapped in old blankets, rags, or whatever could be found to trudge the endless miles. Men had expected to be walking much of the way and stocked themselves with heavy boots. Today, I doubly appreciate mine.

Soon I come upon a circle of stones. Having read the emigrant journals, I quickly recognize the stones as a grave marker. The circle is small, probably an infant's grave.

In poignant simplicity, the ring of stones cries out its story as I kneel to touch the dimpled land. Through a 150-year time warp, suddenly I'm a pioneer mother who's just patted the soil over my baby's tiny body along that lonely trail. I step back. A wail swells my throat as wagons rumble back and forth over the tiny grave in attempt to make it inconspicuous. Dear Lord, how can I allow oxen to lumber over this holy ground? Alas, the choice is not mine.

Frantic, I glance toward the wagon train falling into line and stretching toward the next distant hill. I must go. But leave my baby behind in this God-forsaken place? In this shallow grave where wolves and coyotes howl in the nearby hills? Tears stream down my cheeks. My cold hands clench in fists of anger. I turn away and run stumbling toward the wagons.

Struggling for reality, I'm shaking all over. The trail is much more powerful than I'd expected. My eyes swimming in tears refract a rainbow of color from a patch of pink bitterroot, wild daisies and orange globe mallow growing nearby and it lifts me. I rise to my feet and search the blue-skied distance for my mate.

Soon I see him heading toward me. When we meet, he doesn't share his thoughts or ask mine. Instead, he attempts to lighten the moment with humor.

"I found a souvenir for you," he says, smiling as he hands me a round flat stone about eight inches in diameter. "It's a petrified buffalo chip."

Our laughter sings in the wind. The near-spiritual experience of walking in the footprints of our brave forebears fades into the past like the dimming wagon tracks we've just followed. And I'm so grateful for the trail they blazed for us, the trail to the here and now.

WYOMING'S OREGON TRAIL

I have learned to use the word impossible with the greatest caution.
— *Wernher Von Braun*

Because of the rare courage and sometimes reckless seeming determination of a people to pioneer new territory about 160 years ago, America has grown by leaps and bounds. In Wyoming, where few farm-oriented emigrants elected to remain in that earlier time, cattle and sheep ranches flourish and crops of sugar beets, grain, alfalfa and grass hay are grown in lower elevations to help provide a healthy economy.

Along with agriculture, the state boasts oil, natural gas, mineral and coal production in sizable amounts. Yellowstone Park and many other high country recreation opportunities lure both winter and summertime tourists in numbers early mountain men could never have dreamed of.

High quality educational and medical facilities offer services to all areas of Wyoming or are within reasonable distance of a population scattered over many miles of wide open spaces.

Those spaces, a prime reason that many choose to live here today, inspire and create a culture all its own. Artists, writers, and those who respond to nature on any level, whether fishermen, hunters, backpackers, snowmobilers, skiers, or simply lovers of the outdoors in general suspect the emigrants might have seen all these treasures in a different light had they not been consumed with mere survival.

The American Indian people, who now live on undisputed territory they call "nations," have access to hospitals, highways, schools, libraries and other facilities built by people of all cultures. Many live and work off the reservation as well as on. A growing number are college educated and have become doctors, lawyers, teachers, etc.

Their deep spiritual awareness of humanity's oneness with its environment shares a gentle and valued reminder when people grow too worldly or careless with Earth's gifts.

Today, we ask ourselves, "Was all this change in Wyoming and the development of the west divinely or otherwise destined to happen as many believe?"

How did it affect us as humans? Have we grown? Is what happened inside people as great as what happened outside? And what else is out there? What else is possible?

All these questions and more grow from the amazing trek that created the Oregon Trail and altered hundreds of thousands of lives in a very short period of time.

It happened nearly 160 years ago. Yet the spirit of the pioneer, the adventurer, is still alive and well in Wyoming. Many see a trace of the feisty, intrepid character of the emigrants in themselves today.

To quote one Wyoming resident, "That's why I live here. The challenge allows me to prove what I'm made of."

Maybe that's what the Oregon Trail trek was really about.

Large sink-hole near Sundance, WY, typical of those used by early day Indians for buffalo jump.

Ned Case photo

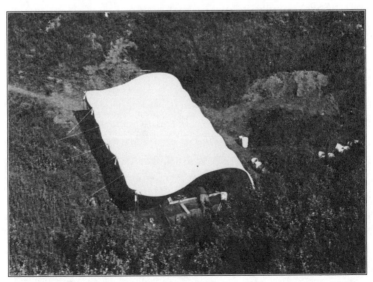

University of Wyoming archeologists work under protective canopy to retrieve buffalo jump artifacts.

Author's photo

A VIVID SLICE OF HISTORY

Life is not dated merely by years. Events are sometimes the best calendars. -Benjamin Disraeli

When I ask people if they've seen the Vore Buffalo Jump near Sundance, a few say "Yes," but too often the answer is, "Never heard of it. What's a buffalo jump?"

It is no less than one of the world's most intriguing archeological sites.

Several years ago, Ned and I felt sure we'd located the jump. Nothing was marked, so we hiked the lush green hills and cocked our ears to the depths of the big sink holes in shifting red soil. In that colorful and haunting place, we pretended to hear spirit calls of the Plains Indians' ancestors, who provided their people with winter food and clothing by stampeding herds of bison into the huge natural vaults for 300 years, between 1500 and 1800 A.D. We heard only an owl hen calling to her chick below.

More recently, on our way to Devils Tower, we noticed two brightly decorated tepees sitting between Highway 90 and an access road that runs parallel to it.

We stopped. There, with little fanfare, but literally sinking into the red earth of the borrow pit beside the busy highway, was the historic Vore Buffalo Jump. No wonder we missed it before. It's too easy to find.

Signs at the top of the huge pit warn of rattlesnakes and poison ivy, should you be brave or curious enough to hike down the curving red clay path to the dig. We couldn't resist. As the sign warned, the three-leafed little plants waved everywhere in deceitful innocence, just a few inches from our feet as we passed. For once, I was grateful for wet and chilly weather. Rattlesnakes offered no challenge.

At the bottom of the sink hole, now covered by a large white canopy, archeologists from the University of Wyoming scraped ever so delicately with small, precise

Layer upon layer of bones in the dig tell the story of Vore Buffalo Jump.

University of Wyoming photo

knives at the rusty gumbo soil. Skeletons of an estimated 20,000 bison lie shrouded by the ages in this communal snare. The bones are scattered throughout an area about 100 feet across and layered nearly 25 feet deep. The scene as well as the history is awesome.

Inside a tent at the top, a painting of the jump in use as envisioned by artist David Paulley had lit my mind's eye. Now I could almost hear the thunder of buffalo hooves beating the path to their death, smell the sweat and the dust as hunters swarmed into the pit with sharpened rocks and bones to butcher the bison amid happy cries of their people who'd be fed and clothed by another successful jump.

This day, we listened to the archeologists' lively and learned response to our questions. They want your imagination, your interest. They want you curious and questioning. It gives them hope.

When Highway 90 was under construction in the 1970s, workers became curious about the green vegetation sinking into a deep red pit near their construction. On investigation, they came upon bones. Lots of bones.

The matter was reported to the Vore family who owned the land. They asked the University of Wyoming to investigate. In 1989, the family of ranchers Woodrow and Doris Vore donated the archeological treasure to the University.

An exploratory excavation created a large vault to determine the extent of the find. Photographs of that dig show bones and artifacts jutting from the walls in profusion, the quality of preservation unmatched anywhere. Because the jump's treasures were buried quickly but gently by nature with thin layers of sediment, they did not decompose or erode away as generally happens.

The vault was temporarily filled for protection, but the dig continues. The University and the Vore Buffalo Jump Foundation hope to build a world class facility to house this precious discovery, making it accessible to the public. They invite membership and contributions. Such construction is expensive and funding difficult to obtain.

This site offers excellent record of ecological change, weather cycles, etc., along with an opportunity to share an uncommon human legacy with the world. Educational potential is great.

I doubt a value could be placed on the Vore Buffalo Jump, either by Native Americans or we who came to join them in this colorful land. A vivid slice of our country's history lies buried there, with mysterious and haunting stories to tell.

The castle-like home he called "Big Teepee," built in Lost Cabin in 1901 by early day Wyoming entrepreneur and sheep rancher J. B. Okie.

Ranger photo

THE BIG TEEPEE

We don't know who we are until we see what we can do.
- Martha Grimes

From Lost Cabin to Big Teepee? John Brognard Okie's homes might better be described, "from dugout to mansion." It was quite a leap.

The original Okie home in 1884 was a simple dugout in the side of the bluffs near Badwater Creek. Soon a log cabin was built, with rooms added as the family grew.

In 1901, rising like a king among poor sageland relatives, the stately residence of wealthy Wyoming sheep rancher J.B. Okie was built in the tiny town of Lost Cabin. Okie jokingly dubbed his castle, "The Big Teepee."

A Fremont County pioneer, J.B.'s intellect and vision were awesome, as proven by his many remarkable achievements. He is said to have had the first telephone, electricity and flush toilets anywhere around. In addition to his very successful sheep ranching operation, he owned grocery stores in several towns and states. In Lost Cabin, he also built a department store, administration building, dance pavilion, hotel and bunkhouse, all sizable structures.

Men employed in Okie's stock operations enjoyed private rooms along with indoor bathrooms and running water. With such facilities, it was said that ranch hands virtually stood in line for work at Okie's Big Horn Sheep Company.

Okie fathered eight children by his first wife, Jeannette, a hard-working, community serving woman who filled medical needs of the area, mainly through home-opathic remedies of her own. Just how such injuries as bull gorings might be treated homeopathically is unknown, but historic accounts say Jeannette dealt with them all.

She apparently had no homeopathic remedy for her philandering man, however. Jeannette lived in the mansion only six years before J.B. divorced her and quickly married a younger woman with whom he traveled the world and purchased fine furnishings for the Big Teepee. Okie later married a third time, fathering two more children.

John Brognard Okie drowned in 1930 at the age of 64, while fishing in a lake near his home. Specific circumstances of the death are unknown.

The famous Okie property was purchased by the Spratt family in 1945, and sold in 1998 to Burlington Resources who today grant occasional visits to the mansion. Guided tours are usually conducted by Fremont County's Riverton Museum Director Loren Jost, a well-known historian, and the mansion's dedicated caretaker, Zane Fross.

Fross, who worked 16 years for the Spratt family is a knowledgeable man who keeps the grounds of the Big Teepee beautifully manicured. Visitors are sometimes invited to bring picnic lunches to eat on a lush green lawn in the shade of heavy-leafed trees. An attractive house for the birds rises above an old clothesline draped with healthy, fruit-bearing grapevines.

A small, fenced and tree lined family cemetery lies not far to the north of the mansion, where Okie, his two sons and his brother lie buried. Instead of the ostentatious markers one might expect in such a place, only small, flat stones mark the four graves. Fross says the original stones which stood erect and distinct, were pushed over the bank of Badwater Creek with permission of the Okie family when the property was purchased by the Spratts. The new owners didn't object to the private burial ground in their yard, but preferred it be less obvious.

Though it might be quite an undertaking, history buffs, including this author, would like to see the original gravestones retrieved and replaced at the burial site to help tell the unique history of this place and its residents.

Today the Big Teepee is attractively decorated throughout with modern day carpeting, but retains some original wallpapers, that in the dining room revealing the Netherlands ancestry of J.B.'s second wife. The living, dining and library rooms each have their original elegant fireplaces and carbide light fixtures.

Visitors are allowed to use the main floor bathroom and two on the second or bedroom level. Beautiful ceramic tiles of floral design line the walls of the baths. Original tubs, washbowls and stools are still in place, in excellent condition and functional.

On the third floor is an attractive cupola one might envision an inspiring room for painting or writing. It was never used for that purpose, however, since in summer it's extremely hot up there. Fross believes the cupola was more likely built as an "eagle nest" for J.B. to observe the behavior of his sheepherders and survey his vast domain.

On the third floor also stands a cistern of which J.B. was said to be quite proud. The huge vessel was filled from a well below where servants pumped endlessly to keep it ready to serve the mansion's needs.

Today, no one lives in the Big Teepee. It's empty of the elegant furnishings and the colorful Okie family. Still, the unique character of the home remains intact and well cared for.

Curator Loren Jost received a number of artifacts for the Riverton Museum when the Spratt family sold the property. He and caretaker Zane Fross plan to resurrect its early residents in future stories and tours as they gain more information for sharing the romantic past of Wyoming's sagebrush castle - the historic "Big Teepee."

* * * * * * * * * *

Other historic mansions of Wyoming include: The Kendrick Mansion in Cheyenne, the Ferris Mansion in Rawlins, and the Governor's Mansion in Cheyenne

Petroglyphs in the Dubois area.

Ned Case photo

Petroglyphs in the Dubois area.

Ned Case photo

PETROGLYPHS: THE TALKING ROCKS

Never assume the obvious is true.   *- William Safire*

Petroglyphs. They're the earliest mystery stories in print.

From our beginnings, we humans have felt a need to express ourselves in some way, and for various reasons. Of necessity, we use materials at hand. Petroglyphs and pictographs are one of the less explained means of expression in this country, generally thought to have been created in Wyoming by Plains Indians. Travelers of the Oregon Trail in the 1840s used a similar method, carving names and dates into The Desert Register, that huge promontory also called Independence Rock. But they spoke our language. The rock art guards its secrets.

Petroglyphs, pictures or images of humans and animals carved, pecked, or incised in stone have been given various names, mostly because no one truly knows what they are, exactly who created them, why or when. They've been estimated to be anywhere from 2,000 to 4,000 years old.

Pictographs are similar shapes painted on stone, usually in black or red colors. The red paint is considered to be iron oxide, a natural element abundant in Wyoming. Charcoal was used for the black, as it is in some types of today's art.

The symbols at more than 200 mysterious sites found so far in Wyoming are thought to have been created with sharp rocks, most often in buff-colored sandstone. The creations have been colorfully characterized as Wyoming's "first documents," "stone art" and "symbols in stone."

As a writer, I think of them as "talking rocks." Communicators. Beside the joy of creating art itself, the messages in stone may have been used, like smoke

Petroglyphs found in Dubois area.

Ned Case photo

signals or the telegraph, as a way of sharing non-verbal information. The symbols may be expressions of ordinary experience, of religious practice, recorded history, or perhaps a means of advising others who might travel the same trail, of the types of food or predators in the area. Some see them as art only, some as early script, and others as a way of passing time.Thus, the glyphs can be more inclusively described as one of the earliest forms of written communication in this land.

"Talking rocks" fits all those possibilities and more. Certainly they've piqued the curiosity of many, and few answers beyond conjecture have so far been found.

The often rectangular-shaped human bodies depicted on the rocks may have been made that way because straight lines were easier to carve in stone. Yet the heads are generally round. Being part artist and creative in thought myself, I wonder if crafters of the rock art might have seen their own reflections in a pond or lake, wind-rippled and shapeless, and assumed a re-creation of self should look that way. It's been noted that the sites are often found near natural water reservoirs of one sort or another.

My venturesome mate and I have explored the enchanting rock art in various parts of Wyoming such as Castle Gardens, Legend Rock, Sinks Canyon, Whiskey Basin, Dinwoody and others, with many sites yet to explore. We've found some petroglyphs dimmed through the years by erosion and algae growth. We hiked across deep, rattlesnake inhabited ravines one hot day to reach a special cluster of tall rocks atop a high hill. Later, on return to that area, we were disappointed to find a huge portion of the early Wyoming outdoor art had broken loose for some reason and fallen to the valley below.

Today, many of us are trying to learn from and preserve these strange recorded symbols of a long ago time and people. The curious works seem a temptation to vandals, and sometimes to artifact hunters. Too late they discover that collection of the elusive art is virtually impossible and only serves to destroy an irreplaceable record of the past. Rocks don't yield their treasures easily.

In attempt to save these historic sites, the U.S. Department of Interior's Bureau of Land Management is working hard to inspect and rescue what is left. Many petroglyph and pictograph sites are now being fenced, access restricted, and some are under lock and key.

Other sites, treasured and protected by Indian people and many of their Caucasian friends, are simply kept secret lest they be destroyed by those who don't appreciate the haunting and uniquely portrayed messages from the past.

If a value could actually be attached to these mystical creations, comparison of sorts might be made with an item seen on television's Traveling Antiques show. A simple store ledger of early day America, filled with art very similar in style to the petroglyphs and pictographs, was valued by highly respected New York City appraisers at $60,000 to $80,000. Each colored drawing had a tiny black horse at the top. The horse was determined by antique experts to be the signature of the Indian artist, Black Horse.

While this information helps us sense what treasures lie about us, it also adds to the mystery of the "talking rocks." And we like mystery. But might we be trying too hard to complicate things?

Indian people were and are often named after animals, birds, parts of the Earth, or events at their birth. Maybe the tiny black horse on the art in the Indian ledger book means our rock stories are simpler than we wish to see them. Maybe, like the Oregon Trail trekkers, the creators of the "talking rocks" were travelers through an area and an era, who, wishing to be a part of something more lasting, simply signed their names and moved on.

Or maybe not.

DAYS OF THE TIE DRIVES

History never looks like history when you're living through it.
- John Gardner

Along with robins, green growth and swelling blossoms, in spring we're reminded of an historic ritual that was part of Wyoming life from the early 1900s to about 1945 - the days of the tie drives.

This remarkable era is recorded in *Knights of The Broadax*, a vivid story of the tie hack days by Joan Trego Pinkerton, who as a teenager witnessed the passing of that important era in American and Wyoming history herself. Her father, A.B. "Treg" Trego served as secretary-bookkeeper for Wyoming Tie & Timber Company, operator of the DuNoir area process. Treg, who also served as postmaster at the site, recorded on film many important images of that unique time and place.

All winter long in those years, lodgepole pines were felled in the Wind River Mountains and hewed into railroad crossties with broadaxes. Tie hacks, the men who did this work, were mostly big Scandinavian men along with some Native and a couple of African Americans, shaping and smoothing the logs into ties within 3/4" of railroad requirements without even measuring them. Along with the hard and dangerous work, came lusty brawls, drinking, and feats of heroism and strength.

Spring thaw brought the big drives. In that area and era, over ten million ties were cut, snaked from the woods and floated down wooden flumes to the Big Wind River. From there, the ties were ridden, guided and prodded on down the river in a spectacular 100-mile drive to the Riverton tie yards.

Pinkerton's book, published in 1981, states that few were alive then who even remembered the tie hacks. Obviously she meant few who remembered them personally, because many Wyomingites have been aware of them and their historic contribution to our country all their lives. Some who participated to a degree in that activity still live in this community and state, probably in the age group of Bob Peck, Ned Case, and Ingebjorg (Aspli) Stork, all in their teens at the time.

In a Riverton Ranger newspaper article, publisher Bob Peck (now Wyoming Senator Peck) wrote of a harrowing 1942 experience when a brave tie hack, Victor Montoya, risked his own life, wading into deep and perilous waters of the Big Wind River to rescue Bob from a raging whirlpool around a fallen tree jammed with ties.

My husband, Ned, in his late teens drove a truck for Ross Bisbee, hauling oats to feed the 40 work horses used to snake logs from the wooded mountain down to Warm Springs Creek and the flumes. This was in 1940-41, shortly before the entire process was mechanized. Backhauls brought lumber from Dubois area mills to customers in the lowlands.

This hard and dangerous life was further complicated by language differences. A story is told in Pinkerton's book of Ingebjorg's father, Oscar Aspli, a young Norwegian who left his wife Dorothea and baby daughter behind when he came to work in Wyoming in 1926. When he was finally able to send for them 10 years later, his speech had become such a strange conglomeration of Norwegian, Swedish and English that his wife couldn't understand a word he said.

Another story tells of Bill Brown, an articulate black tie hack who quickly became fluent in the Swedish language. Bill enjoyed explaining to the awed and trusting immigrants, "If you stay in this country as long as I have, you'll turn black, too!"

Many believed him.

According to Pinkerton's book, many of the Scandinavian men intended to bring their wives and familes to this country as soon as they'd saved enough money. Whether because their earnings fell victim to booze or that they felt this life too rough for their families, few saw that day come to pass. What they experienced instead was years of rough and dangerous work while they carved from Wyoming's mountains a critical part of America's railroad system.

Of the women who did immigrate to this country and share in that unusual life, however, their memories were expressed with the words, "Those were the best years of my life!"

After Ned and I married, when we drove to the mountains to fish we often examined the deteriorating old wooden flumes on Warm Springs Creek to see how they could have functioned as a water-driven conveyor of tumbling ties. Parts of the flume can still be seen today, if you know what to look for. I remember one where trout liked to hide in its cool shadows.

We used to drive by the old Wyoming Tie and Timber Company camp buildings in the DuNoir area and imagine what life was like for people in that time and setting. The buildings have long since been torn down.

Many of the ties created in those days were used in maintaining the Chicago & Northwestern Railroad that once ran through Riverton. Another Ranger clipping from my files tells a poignant story by then editor Dave Perry, with photos of the last run of the C&NW train through Riverton on those ties on September 15, 1988.

When Ned and I moved back to Wyoming and Pheasant Crest Farm in 1982, we framed our yard with railroad ties. One was clearly hand-hewn. We were pleased to realize it quite likely came from the tie drives of the early 1940s when Bob Peck, Ned and others of our generation played some part in their origin.

Today, the lives and contributions of the rough and revered "Knights of The Broadax" are commemorated by a 14-foot high limestone monument surrounded by railroad ties, standing on a knoll on Highway 26 west of Dubois. The monument, erected in 1947, overlooks the site of the first tie camp.

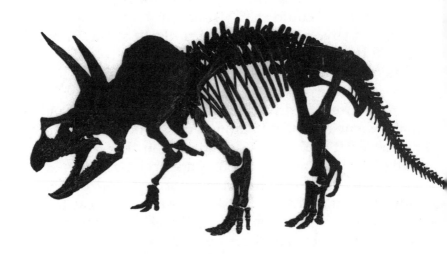

A three-horned triceratops horridus is one of 12 full skeletons on display at Wyoming Dinosaur Center in Thermopolis.

Wyoming Dinosaur Center photo

DINOSAURS: THE EARLY BIRDS

There is no square on earth as rich as Wyoming in its fossil forms of life. Nearly all the life that ever lived upon Earth can be found within the limits of this state.
- Curator William H. Reed, University of Wyoming - 1899.

"Today you can be a visitor; 150 million years ago you would have been a snack," reads the clever road sign alerting travelers to the Wyoming Dinosaur Center in Thermopolis.

It's all for fun, of course. 150 million years ago, you wouldn't have been available as a snack. Unless, of course, your name was Fred Flintstone and you lived in Gondwanaland, a part of which later became known as Wyoming. On second thought, I don't believe Fred was that old, either.

It's hard for those of us who lived here B.D. to believe the huge creatures once really walked our land. (B.D. means Before Discovery, not Before Dinosaurs, by the way.) How could we have dreamed these ancient animals were buried by the hundreds or even thousands right under our feet?

When we were teenagers, "Thermop" was the place to go. Cars and gasoline were hard for youth to come by in those days. A drive through scenic Wind River Canyon, with the road snaking along a wide blue-green river walled by 2,000 foot cliffs on both sides, was awesome. The canyon's three dark tunnels offered a chance to yell or honk the horn and hear the walls answer back. In contrast to most of Wyoming, where wide open spaces allow echoes no chance to respond, we never missed this one. In Thermopolis, it was a thrill to stroll around the rainbow painted hot springs, swim in a warm plunge, and drive up the hill to watch the buffalo herd grazing the red and green hills.

To we who thought this colorful place a land of

enchantment as it was then, it's sheer wonder to learn that a veritable Jurassic Park population lay sleeping all around us; that for 160 million years before man arrived, those giant creatures ruled this very land.

It's also hard to figure out just where "this very land" was in dinosaur days. Geologists believe the shifting soil we now call Wyoming was likely a lush tropical area called Gondwanaland nearer the equator, about where Mexico lies today, hot and humid.

The word dinosaur in Greek means "terrible lizard." Of course these creatures were not lizards, but the huge meat-eaters were indeed terrible, often standing at a height of 20 feet, with four-foot long skulls and great dagger-like teeth. The biggest plant eating dinosaurs were 90 feet long and weighed as much as 85 tons.

As the land shifted north and mountains rose from the Earth, the great creatures' swampland homes dried up, along with their plant food. Since some of the dinosaurs, the herbivores, ate plants and the others, the carnivores, ate the ones that ate the plants, the balanced food chain gradually disappeared. That process is estimated to have taken between 10 million and 20 million years.

The discovery of these amazing deposits occurred almost by accident in 1992 when Ulrich (Uli) Leonhardt and Burkhard Pohl, paleontologists from Germany made a private visit to Wyoming. Searching for fossils, they contacted a longtime fossil hunter, Eddy Cole, Sr. from Delta, Utah, who noted a "promising look" to the Morrison formation in the ridges near Thermopolis. Further exploration in the summer of 1993 led to the discovery of dinosaur bones on the Warm Springs Ranch near Thermopolis, and the property was purchased by Pohl and his associates that fall.

The discoveries are even more amazing to the people who lived on the land than to we who celebrated our youth there.

Lonnie, the widow of one-time ranch owner Bud Jones, says, "I've ridden horses all over the ranch and never had a clue about there being any dinosaur remains there."

Her brother-in-law, Dennis Jones, who grew up on the ranch, explains why. "Where the beds were discovered is an area where no self-respecting cow would go," he says. "And we went where the cattle went."

Since the property was purchased in 1993 by Dr. Pohl's company, Big Horn Prospecting, Inc., Dr. Richard Bersch has come from Germany to assist on a temporary basis and shares the company along with Pohl and Uli Leonhardt. Wyoming geologist Michael T. (Ty) Naus, the most pursued geologist in his college graduating class of 1993, joined the group and became chief geologist and paleontological consultant to Big Horn Prospecting, Inc.

The Wyoming Dinosaur Center, a 16,000 foot complex, opened in 1995 just two miles out of Thermopolis. Giant dinosaur tracks painted on the streets lead visitors to the museum displaying many kinds of prehistoric creatures. To date, 21 different dinosaurs have been found at the dig sites nearby. Dinosaur bones from the U.S. and some foreign countries are displayed in the museum as well as various other types of fossils and information.

Over 50 places on the Warm Springs ranch show signs of dinosaur fossils. Uncovering the bones is difficult and tedious but exciting work. Bones are not found above ground, though footprints in stone may lead scientists to a productive dig. Bones must be excavated very carefully with small tools and brushes, then removed, marked and transported to the museum's lab where additional cleaning, identification and cataloging is done.

A cast of the second-largest tyrannosaurus rex ever found, and the most complete T-rex ever discovered, is the highlight of the center's display, standing 15 feet high at the shoulder. Even with a skull 5 feet long, "Stan," as he's been named, appears to have led a very rough life. Broken bones and other serious injuries to his face, neck, ribs and skull tell the story of probable battle with other similar creatures.

The original T-rex bones were found near Buffalo, S.D., but precise casts were made of each bone to create "Stan." Casts are often used for displays because they're lighter in weight and easier to move, but nonetheless accurate.

In gentle contrast to the great tyrannosaurus-rex, a little wooden rocking horse named "Rock-a-Saurus Rex" stands in a safer spot for small children to enjoy, bringing a smile and a light touch to the almost overwhelming size of most inhabitants of this place.

The giant beasts disappeared mysteriously from Earth about 65 million years ago, long before man made his appearance. But the dinosaurs left enough evidence of their early presence in this part of Wyoming to keep pale-ontologists curious and busy for another 200 to 300 years.

Like an ongoing mystery story, the ancient crea-tures reveal their secrets one at a time. As recently as April in the year of 2000, scientists were amazed to discover that some of the dinosaurs long thought to be reptiles are not. A new manner of x-ray revealed that at least one branch of the dinosaur family had a heart with four chambers and one aorta - very similar to humans.

HIGH COUNTRY VIEWS

How It Looks from Here -

Among the many things I've learned from life in Wyoming, there's one I most treasure: An awareness and awe of the creative force itself, the energy that builds and powers the universe; knowing I move in its flow, can choose to walk in its most shallow waters or wade the mysterious depths. The following pieces speak that understanding, some light-hearted and playful, others drawn from a deeper perception of life's mysteries and meanings.

AN AVALANCHE OF PAPER

"Don't they have anything to read?" Ned asked after we'd visited in someone else's home.

I hadn't noticed papers and books around that home, either. But I suspect my mate's view is a little warped. After all, he's lived with me a long time.

Someday I fully expect to disappear under a paper avalanche. Believe me, there'd be plenty of fuel for cremation. Maybe even spontaneous combustion.

This problem may be traceable to my childhood. Paper didn't arrive then to fill one's mailbox daily with boxholders, sales and solicitations as it does today. In fact, paper was a precious material.

The walls inside our house were covered with it. Not beautiful flower-strewn wallpaper, but a heavy, functional building paper, with only a vague hint that its manufacturer thought of pattern or color.

The paper came in huge rolls and my father fastened it over the entire inside of our house with big-headed tacks to keep out winter cold. Even then on a December morning, we could scrape at least an eighth-inch of frost from the big tack heads.

Our neighbor's walls were covered with newspapers. At the time, I thought it quite strange. But the tiny woman chuckled, "Why not? There's plenty of reading material handy, and pictures to look at all through the house."

I now think of her as a born survivor.

Although my grandfather was a newspaper publisher, we never considered pasting his work on our walls for insulation. But he often had a hand in the decorating.

Memories of childhood burst with color when I recall shoe boxes of paper that Grandpa sent from time to time. This wasn't newspaper, or even something for sketching. It was bright colored strips trimmed from sale bills he'd printed. I'm sure it would have been easier to just let the excess fall into the waste basket. But grandpas aren't made that way.

When the pretty pastel rolls of pink, blue, yellow and green arrived, Mother stirred up flour paste and my sisters and I created beautiful paper chains to decorate our little house on the South Dakota prairie. For a while, we'd live in a real carnival atmosphere. Eventually, spider webs filled the colorful circles and Mother informed us they'd be impossible to dust.

As a child, my artistic leanings demanded attention. One day, while poring over Mother's college textbooks hoping I'd discover a magic key to the German language, I noticed a flyleaf. A beautiful, naked flyleaf.

Here was a blank page of high quality paper serving no earthly purpose at all.

Did I dare ease it loose? Would Mother recognize it? Would she miss it? Once removed, I couldn't put it back.

Somehow, the page gradually let go of its well-sewn spine and fell into my lap. What could I do now but use it? If I didn't, it would be wasted.

When my drawing was finished, I had to work up courage to ask Mother's opinion of my work. Her response was generally positive, but when I hadn't done so well, she'd say gently, "I'm not artistic, but this part doesn't seem quite right. Why don't you try again?"

Inside, I was quivering. This could require another flyleaf. Another chance she'd recognize the paper. After all, books are important to a school teacher.

Eventually, all of Mother's college textbooks yielded their flyleaves to my art. When she was 86, I asked, "Mother why didn't you say anything? Surely you guessed where my art paper came from?"

"No," she insisted, giving me a blank look. "Never thought about it."

It's not too hard to see how my paper trail was built. Nobody ever said, "Halt the construction."

And Ned, after following me down that path for so many years, has come to suppose ours is a normal home. Ah well, he could have followed a woman down a yellow brick road . . . . .

FACT AND FAITH IN THE NEW YEAR

Recently, I read an article by a woman who said she felt there was nothing magical about the start of a new year, no added motivation. If we think of it that way, how can there be motivation? The new year certainly doesn't lack incentive for me.

For one thing, January allows me to start looking toward spring instead of winter. And though I know spring is still down the line a way, warmer temperatures have been teasing at us from all around the state. A few days of sunshine in our hometown have been most welcome and I have faith that even better days lie ahead.

But spring isn't all that can inspire. First, there's today. This morning. This hour. This minute. I intend to make use of it all.

The woman also lamented that she had a poor history when it comes to resolutions. I wonder if she simply suffers a weakness of faith in life, a failure to view life in a positive, hopeful way.

I wished she could have been in our church last Sunday when our pastor challenged us with the question, "Where are we going?" While focused on the spiritual, the differences between faith and fact opened new avenues of thought.

"What you believe has more to do with what happens than fact," the pastor emphasized. "Your five senses discern fact, but faith overrides the senses."

I thought on this statement. I jotted it down on my program. Applied faith does affect today's living.

My mate was driving to Cheyenne that afternoon. I felt some concern that he was driving alone. My senses told me that while the sun was shining then, weather in southeastern Wyoming can change quickly and make travel quite treacherous. My faith told me he would drive safely. He'd stop if he got sleepy, if he needed a cup of coffee from the thermos.That evening he phoned to tell me he'd arrived at his motel in Cheyenne. I could have worried about it, but that would change nothing. Faith kept me calm.

I stayed home because I had writing deadlines to meet. My senses told me I had no subject for my next column. My faith told me one would come. My senses tell me time is running out on my declared publication date for my new book. My faith tells me if I work diligently, it will come together as planned.

Positive thinking and success are born of faith. Granted, our senses provide a reality essential to physical survival. But the strength of faith gets us where we want to go.

Our pastor's message included the fact that we must exercise faith lest it deteriorate like an unused muscle. Lack of faith in the positive and hopeful weakens. It lends strength to the negative and failure moves in.

At a New Year's gathering at our home, the conversation, sometimes laced with concern about younger family members, leaned toward how to keep the new in the new year. The subject of worry came up. One couple said they'd heard that worry is "praying to yourself."

What a peculiar idea, I thought. But I found it challenging and I thought again.

If you're going to undermine yourself with what might happen, how can there be any room for faith in what can happen?

Yes, worry has about as much potential as praying to yourself.

So, back to the woman who saw no added motivation to the start of a new year. If she's clinging to past fact without faith, I thought, expecting to fail in her new year's resolutions, she may be right. If she expects to see nothing inspiring, that's what she will find.

But if faith tells us there's more fact to life than last fall's killing frost, more than cold, icy weather ahead, then hope for the future is born.

The rosebush under the box outside my window understands that.

THE CLONING TRAIL

When a Scottish scientist discovered that all life needs to copy itself is cells from the breast of the female, implanted in her unfertilized egg, incubated in her womb, the first mammal was cloned–a sheep the scientists named Dolly.

My first response was concern for her creators. Where does this leave the male role in reproduction? Could man make himself obsolete? Design himself out of existence? I'm not too happy with the thought. I sort liked the species.

"This same technique might make it possible to clone humans," said the experts. "Though we consider it unethical to try."

Ethical or not, it's a great temptation. I suspect it won't be long until some scientist has to prove he can do it and claim the dubious fame of being the first to accomplish this feat.

My dictionary defines a clone as "a group of organisms derived from a single individual by asexual reproduction." If it's asexual, why does it have so much to do with one sex, the female? Asexual means lacking sex. The deeper I get into this thing, the more confusing it becomes. But like the scientists, how can I stop here?

Since this process as presently proven successful involved only female parts, can the male be cloned? Does he have the necessary equipment? From where would his cloning cells come? And would it be a truly male clone if the egg and womb of the female were involved?

The first release I read from the Associated Press states that "The (cloning) process was horrendously inefficient." Not surprising. The old reproduction process seems rather popular. And so efficient that we've over-populated much of the Earth. But we were getting to the point we could handle that, if we would.

One thing I'm glad about in all this is that it was a male scientist who created the ewe clone. If it had been a female, she might be suspected of attempting to build a race of Amazonian feminists, agreeing deep in their genes on the future of this world.

Another thought, and I recognize this as a far reach too: If the world's population were created by cloning, would there be no wars? We might lose patience with our "other selves," but we don't usually respond violently when we realize we've made a dumb mistake.

In this iffy realm, questions beget questions. Without disagreement, and if there were no differences of sex, behavior, opinion, how would we ever be challenged? Learn anything new? What would there be to explore? And wouldn't this life be dull?

I confess I've taken this great scientific discovery on a wild trip. But I hope male scientists recognize the potential of their minds to destroy as well as create. Men could head their own endangered species list. I thought it rather nice to have them a part of the process of life. I don't need another "me" and I don't need another "him." I like the two of us just as we are.

A final and very serious thought on human cloning comes from Karen Rothenberg of the National Advisory Board on Ethics and Reproduction. "Do we really want to alter the dignity of what it means in our souls to be human?

I hope we'll think on these things.

MID-LIFE MARRIAGE

Have you noticed that people in wedding pictures in the newspapers look more mature these days? I can recall when only fresh young faces filled most wedding announcements. Still, a mid-life marriage can carry all the magic of an early one, and possibly more potential for success.

When we attended the wedding of our son to a lovely and talented woman, the union seemed right from the start.

"I wish they could have met earlier in life," I comment to our son's father.

"Maybe it's more important that they found each other now," he replies.

The response stirs my thoughts. Might it be that when people have prior and perhaps painful experience as a reference, love takes on deeper meaning?

Like the rest of us, our son has changed. He values different things than he used to. No doubt she does too.

"I've waited 17 years for him," she says.

What a beautiful line.

To me, she's an old-fashioned girl in a contemporary woman. She takes her career seriously. She's also a gourmet cook who loves to prepare and serve delicious food. She does it almost as gracefully over a campfire as in a kitchen.

"I'm not accustomed to this," her future husband says. "I've been a bachelor for a while, but I may be able to adjust quite easily."

An obvious sense of thoughtfulness and appreciation speak of maturity, of honor students in the class of emotional development.

"She's so good to me," he says.

"It's easy when someone's good to you," she explains.

If they remember this, I thought, these two could graduate from life Phi Beta Kappa.

The day before the wedding, his future father-in-law says with a mischievous grin, "You'd better go out and do what you want today. It's your last chance."

Our son looks contemplative. "Strange," he says, "I can't think of anything."

No wild oats to sow, no traces to kick over, no bachelor party. Only a sure and steady desire to see their lives combined.

Twin boys, an important part of this picture, are high school seniors with plans for college coming up.

"We're glad you're marrying him," they tell their mother. "Now we won't have to worry about you."

She's taken aback. "Do teenage boys really worry about a single mom?" she asks.

Maybe more than you know, dear one. And perhaps they're a little more grown up than they sometimes seem.

At rehearsal, there's light-hearted teasing and laughter.

"Who gives this woman?" the pastor asks.

Her entire family jumps up and shouts, "We do!" As if they can't wait.

But on the wedding day, things take a strange turn. Reality is upon us. Today, this is "Baby Sister" we're talking about. And "Mom."

"Who gives this woman?"

A scatter of whispered and low-spoken "we do"s is barely audible in the little church.

The vows are spoken, rings lovingly exchanged, and a large blue union candle lit from smaller ones held by the bride and groom. They turn from the altar, man and wife.

"You may kiss the bride . . ."

He does and she giggles.

A tear of joy blurs my vision. The magic still lives. Love and marriage are more precious than ever before. Maybe partly because these two didn't find each other until mid-life.

UNSEEN AND UNHEARD

We all have strange days. There are "bad hair days," "false start days," and "klutzy days."

But did you ever feel you were invisible or inaudible for all of one day? It's a weird sensation. You feel like a lost child. Like maybe you should scream, wave a flag, or throw a fit. The latter I almost did. Several times. And there's still no explanation for that day.

To begin, my mate had gone to Casper to attend a four-day insurance seminar. The seminar nearing completion, I phoned very early in the morning to see when he'd arrive back in Riverton, since he'd ridden with someone else.

I dialed. The phone rang. I heard it lifted from the hook, then promptly hung up. I dialed again.

"Thanks for the wake-up call," he responded pleasantly, then quickly replaced the phone on the hook.

On the third try, the second I heard it leave the hook, I shouted, "It's me, Ned! It's me!" This time he listened. His eardrum may never be the same.

This was just the beginning of an eight-hour period when I almost wasn't seen or heard. Clearly, this was a non-Betty day.

At a scheduled appointment, I waited more than 90 minutes to be seen. Finally, with my back and legs cramping from sitting so long, I rose to my feet to stretch. The receptionist apparently thought I was about to leave and quickly pulled my file from the bottom of a large pile and placed it on top.

Why was it on the bottom? I'd checked in an hour and a half ago. Was I phasing in and out of other people's reality? Or did I just think I was manifested in this realm? I'm not very big. Maybe I was shrinking. Might I shrink clear out of existence?

All that day, cars darted out from stop signs to turn left into my lane, right in front of me. I had to move quickly to the other lane to avoid being hit. Was my car invisible too?

In another business place, I stood at a counter waiting to pick up some items. Attendants were quite busy, but I was passed by time after time as others came in after me. A man working across the counter directly in front of me moved repeatedly to wait on others as if I just wasn't there.

At last, a young woman came by and asked, "Have you been waited on?" Apparently, I'd finally phased back into human view. I'm afraid I snapped at the woman and I'm not proud of that. It's just so frustrating to be invisible.

Heading home, my day took on an upbeat tone when I stopped at a grocery store. Moving down the aisle, a man bumped me quite hard from behind with his cart.

"Oh, I'm sorry," he said. "I just didn't see you. Are you okay?"

"I'm fine," I said. I didn't really expect to be seen, but he was so polite and nice, I followed up with a smile and added, "At least I didn't topple into your cart."

The man grinned. All male and all class, he flung back, "Good thing you didn't. I'm not sure I could afford you."

At last. I was finally in sight of someone, however flawed that vision might be.

By the time I got home, Ned was there and quite happy to acknowledge my presence. My invisible day faded into the twilight.

I've read of "out-of-body" experiences, but I was sure I was in mine. I'd even swear it was in this realm. So why did others have so much trouble seeing and hearing me all of one day?

Maybe I'm a ready-made script for Unsolved Mysteries.

MY FATHER NEVER TOLD ME

"My father never told me he loved me."

These are the tearful words of a man I read about not long ago. The funeral was over and he'd never heard the precious words he so longed to have his father speak. I wonder how many children of today's world will never even know their fathers, much less hear them utter those words.

My father never told me he loved me.

But I remember him making up poems about his children when I was small, each one personalized in perfect rhyme and rhythm. Could that be where I first heard the beauty and music of words?

My father never told me he loved me.

But he reached into his pocket one day and handed me all the money he had. After high school, I decided I wanted to attend an educational institution in another state. An aunt and uncle sent money for tuition and books and I'd arranged to work for my room and board. When I told my dad I was leaving, he reached into his pocket and pulled out something like $43 in bills.

"Here," he said. "I'm sorry I can't give you more. This is all I have."

He didn't mean just in his pocket. It was all he had. Period. And he'd just handed it to me.

My father never told me he loved me.

When my mother nearly lost her life in an auto accident, I flew to take my turn staying with my father and helping where needed. In the night, I heard him walking the floor and came up from my basement bedroom to see if he was all right. Before heading back to my room, I planted a kiss on his soft, lined cheek.

"Good night, my good little girl," he said.

My memory spun. These were the words I'd heard every night as a child many years before.

My father never told me he loved me.

While driving to the hospital one morning to see

Mother, I offered advice. He didn't want it. We quarreled. Some things he simply needed to do alone, if only to prove to himself that he could.

Finally, he stopped the car. A muscled arm came around me. His voice quivered.

"I'm sorry."

"Me too."

My father never told me he loved me?

When my generation was growing up, fathers had to give most of their energy to providing food, shelter and clothing for a family, often supplied in the simplest form. Still, a dad was generally there, and children were aware of his presence and strengths even if he didn't or couldn't put his caring into precise words.

When he was tired or worried, sometimes he was grouchy. Sometimes, you even caught a glimpse of his weakness and realized he was as human as yourself.

Seems to me a father's role is increasing in importance these days with rather obvious consistency. Whether they're absent from their children's lives due to divorce, women believing men aren't necessary beyond impregnation, work taking priority, or because they just don't care, reality is painting a tragic picture of life without fathers in this country. Kids scream their need in floundering, destructive behavior.

We all know children who are raised by mothers alone. It's a hard and frightening job. And who knows what the youngsters feel?

Golfer Tiger Woods and basketball's Michael Jordan insist they succeeded because they had loving supportive fathers as well as caring mothers. These men and their parents are some of the best family examples in the world today.

Words of love are always beautiful to hear when sincerely spoken. We're learning it's not so hard to say them. But words need action to give them life, and we must remember that love speaks in many ways. Words of approval, a hug, a warm smile, an act of caring, these gestures and more may relay the message.

In today's hurried world, work, worry and stress can overshadow acts of love. We need to watch for them, lift them out of the busy-ness of our lives and savor them. It's a far better choice than lamenting, "My father never told me."

MISS PIGGY AND THE STEM CELL

I hate to confuse your day, your week, your life, but here's something it's time we consider: Maybe Miss Piggy is a real live being, after all. Maybe she's simply ahead of her time.

She looks like a pig, sort of, but behaves like a flirty, flippant human female. Just one smart crack from a macho male, (she sees them all as macho but can't help flirting, anyway) and her long blond curls bounce in indignation that matches her mouth. Is this fascinating swinelike creature alive? Or is she just a puppet? (Don't take this too lightly, it's going to get deep pretty quick.)

You've probably read or heard on television that scientists have identified the embryonic stem cell, our single cell beginning that in just a couple of weeks divides itself into other cells to become our various body parts, from skin to heart to brain, from kidneys, to lungs to eyes. It's both awesome and frightening.

This discovery has a good side. A very good one. We may soon be able to grow new body parts as well as repair for ailing ones. Researchers are trying to learn how to nudge stem cells toward becoming the specialized tissue needed for regeneration of muscle, bones, nerves, etc. We could grow tissue for testing drugs, then animals may no longer have to give their lives to save ours. We can also create horrible havoc.

Scientists, for all their miraculous discoveries that help us, seem sorely tempted to manipulate life to whatever extent it is within their power. According to a recent news magazine article, the federal government is still on the sidelines regarding this type of development. So far, there is only minimal oversight of this crucial science that's heading society toward unknown dilemmas in the world of genetics. That's scary.

It is suggested that the unscrupulous might even attempt to create human-animal hybrids. Yuk! The very thought throws me into sarcasm. Maybe we could slowly revert ourselves to animals of simple intellect. Maybe we could crawl back into the sea and prove the theory of evolution.

And if we move backward far enough into creation, what if we encounter our Creator, Himself? What will happen to us then? Will we all just go "POOF" as God's miracle of life collapses into itself? Further, would He even be interested in birthing us again?

I remember reading years ago that cartoonists' imaginations often unknowingly forecast the future. If you're old enough, you might remember the Buck Rogers comic strip. I'd like to say Buck was a character from my parents' childhood, but he wasn't. He was from mine. That was before computers and humans on the moon were seriously thought of by anyone but cartoonists, a matter that doesn't prove I'm ancient, just that things happen fast in this life.

Anyway, Buck, in a space suit a bit more sleek and handsome than the ones our astronauts wear, zoomed up into the ether, walking in space, his excursions controlled with a small computer-like tool, sometimes embedded in his wristwatch, where he either punched buttons or simply spoke to a receptor. Sound hauntingly familiar? Don't laugh too hard at Miss Piggy.

One mysterious discovery in this new scientific work is that all stem cells of life are the same. In other words, every living thing on Earth is related in some very basic way that we often ignore. To me, that begs a respect we might work on. Maybe it explains my long felt sense that trees are partly human. Maybe it explains our son's lifelong tendency to help an insect out of his home instead of stepping on it. Maybe we're coming into a clearer and more sensitive understanding of our commonality with all creation.

Wait a minute. Do I see Miss Piggy flipping her blond curls and lifting her round, blunt nose in haughty disgust? "Whaddaya mean, 'just a puppet'? What ever made you think I'd accept commonality with the rest of you, anyway?"

* * * * * * * * * * *

In early 2000, the age of irony arrived. A sow named Destiny gave birth through cloning to five little pigs.

"Pigs are physiologically one of the closest animals to humans," said the Scottish scientists responsible for the cloning. "It raises hopes for a new source of transplants."

"Humph!" (Miss Piggy is back.) "Not my organs! I'm uncloneable."

She probably is. But would you allow a physician to transplant a pig's heart into your body? We discussed it at our house and the first response was a resounding, "No!" Still, what if Miss Piggy's cloned relatives were your last and only hope?

"Don't be so uppity," Miss Piggy snorts. "I told you before I might not accept commonality with you, anyway. My heart would probably reject your body."

Miss Piggy has a good sense of self. Don't put it down. With her heart, you might lose all that insecurity and see youself in a new light.

I can't imagine why male scientists are into this thing. Don't they realize that cloning females with no male involvement could make them obsolete? Has their curiosity overpowered their sex drive? And if that isn't alarming enough, please note that all the piglets are girls. So is Dolly, the sheep cloned earlier by these same scientists.

Isn't that rather scary? Why has there been no concern voiced by either the scientists or the rest of the male population?

"Or by the female population?" interjects Miss Piggy. "I have to line guys out on occasion, but life wouldn't be any fun without them."

Dave Ayares, president of research for PPL Therapeutics of Edinburgh, Scotland, the company that cloned both Dolly the sheep and Destiny's piglets, is serious. Apparently, their scientists believe we humans will be ready and willing recipients of swine body parts.

Isn't it a strange turn of events that the animal

considered the lowliest and most unclean by humans might now become our last hope for life?

And where are the animal rights people in all this?

"There's always a reason given to validate these Frankenstein-like experiments," says Lisa Lange, a spokeswoman for People for The Ethical Treatment of Animals. "Animals are not test tubes with tails, and they are not commodities to be marketed."

"Hear! Hear!" shouts Miss Piggy, flipping her blond curls and lifting her round, blunt nose once more in haughty agreement. "Leave my egg cells alone. Keep your petri dish away from my chromosomes. Stay out of my helix and my DNA, and for heaven sakes, don't try to alter my nucleus! Now. Have I made myself clear?"

Talk about irony. One way or another, Miss Piggy may save us yet.

A LIVING CHAIR

I sit in the old oak rocking chair in our bedroom. A warm sun pushes its rays through the white lace curtains of windows that reach from ceiling to floor. Light lays an arabesque pattern across the pearl gray carpet. Outside the window under a box, a deep red rose waits for spring.

My grandmother's rocker seems to belong in this scene, its back deeply carved with the head of a cherub, her hair flowing in long tendrils to the sides. But was Grandma Satira a lady of lace and curls? Or more like the gutsy rose that defied frost after frost last fall?

I don't remember this paternal ancestor and I feel deprived. I'm told I saw her once, or she saw me, when I was three months old. She died the following year. I've heard she was feisty. Outspoken. Determined. She operated a boarding house, a bed and breakfast type establishment of the late 1800s, while Grandpa was away on carpenter jobs.

Today, my mind is filled with questions. Did Grandma like this chair? Did it fit her character, her body, the way it wraps around my own? Did she buy it herself? Or did Grandpa gift his love with a chair that fit her as he saw her?

My father told me he was rocked in it when a baby, as were his eight brothers and sisters. So too, were my seven siblings and I. Often, several of us would pile our little bodies into it until the arms could hold no more. Then we'd sway forward and back until the chair began to rock. As our appreciation of momentum grew, the chair gained speed. Occasionally, it would reach the end of its rockers and topple, dumping its shrieking load to the floor.

I don't recall any passenger injuries, but the chair sports several mended rungs and spindles, some hand-carved by my father, some probably by his.

"What are you going to do about this old chair?" my father asked as he prepared to move from the big farm house into a smaller home in town. "If you don't want it, it's going on the sale bill."

My heart sank. Sell it? Sell this chair? This living chair?

"The auctioneer wants it himself," my father added, carefully watching my reaction.

What could the chair possibly mean to an auctioneer, I wondered. Age-wise, it probably is antique. But with several original parts replaced, it could never qualify.

"Of course I want the chair!" I exclaimed. Yes, it was old. Some might consider it decrepit. But it was my heritage, my only connection to the grandmother I never knew.

Back in our own home, my husband offered to refinish and restore the little chair, replace its worn, flattened rockers, give it a shiny new coat. I wouldn't hear of it.

How could I let him remove the sweat of my father's hands? The flour from the palms of my spunky grandmother? The sawdust from my carpenter grandfather's clothes?

For several years, I refused to consider restoration. Finally, I recognized what in some way I must have known all along. The old chair's legacy lay in the experiences it shared, not in physical matter.

The cherub-backed rocker is refinished now. The long hair still trails in graceful tendrils to the sides. My husband's hand has added to the mended rungs and spindles. New, long-lasting oak rockers were formed by a disabled Arkansas carpenter. The more human hands touch it, the more the chair seems a living thing.

Now, my mate rises from bed each morning and moves to the comfortable seat to pull on his clothes. After breakfast, I pick up my notebook and pen. I'm drawn by an unseen force to the aged piece of furniture that ties me to my ancestors.

Grandma Satira's spirit calls from the spunky red rose. Her son gave me determination, and poetry, and imagination, and laughter, and yes, a tongue that must sometimes curb itself.

My pen moves confidently across the page. My heritage speaks.

WHEN SPRING TAKES WING

Every year I wonder for weeks, is it spring or isn't it? Our son's birthday heralds the first official day of that magical season, so I always expect sunshine and flowers and singing birds to appear within one day as he did. (My mate reminds me it took nine months, but mothers tend to forget the uncomfortable parts of the process.)

While I wait for a slow-coming spring in Wyoming, I consider tasks like wallpapering bathrooms and cleaning closets.

"You shouldn't keep anything in your closet you haven't worn in the past year," goes the old saying. Does that mean I could part with that short red cheerleader skirt from high school days? And the dress shoes that have come into style for the second time?

My mate's call yanks me back to today's world. "Did you order the master bathroom wallpaper? It will soon be time for serious yard work to begin."

"I'll check to see if it's here," I hedge. Did I order it? Or just think I did? The phone rings. My order is in.

The two of us have wallpapered bathrooms, hallways and such since we married years ago. I view it as the ultimate test of whether a couple truly wants to live together. A periodic exposure to stress helps clarify the commitment.

I'm a perfectionist and he's a "let's get it done" type. That, I figure, is nature's way of keeping a balance. You can guess how it goes. He tells a friend, "I might have to paste her to the wall." I remind him of the woman who wrapped a strip of wet wallpaper around her husband's head.

Before long we're wondering where our brains were when we chose this pattern. Was it really intended to match? And where was our foresight when we designed this bathroom with all the angles, crooks and crannies? Couldn't a rectangular room with only four corners have had as much charm?

When I think we're all done with the job and marvel that we still kiss each other goodnight, he says with a smirk, "We missed a spot. You didn't even notice."

"Where?" I search the room.

"Here." He points to a small area above the door in the recessed area where the stool hides in modest seclusion.

I cut two more pieces of wallpaper, dampen them, and he slaps them on the wall.

"I considered just leaving it," he confesses. "But some day you'd notice and I'd have to drag all this stuff out again."

"You got it, babe," I respond, bringing nature's balancing act into evidence one more time.

That evening we celebrate the successful completion of our job. We note with laughter that I'm not pasted to the wall and he doesn't wear a wallpaper mask. And decorating our bathroom with flowers and birds didn't lure spring weather to Wyoming in March.

Next day an icy blast roars out of the north and shoots pain through my overworked joints. My mate rubs Aspercreme on my shoulders and I apply spiritual salve with a poem I wrote a while back. It reminds me there's reason for both order and disorder in a season of change and rebirth.

The poem, called "Rancher's Spring," goes like this:

> He sets the fence posts in a row;
> puts each one carefully in place;
> they stand like sentinels aligned,
> - except for one, it lays askew -
> a bluebird's nesting at its base.

Yes, I must wait on the order of things. A fledgling needs time to grow feathers before it can fly from the foot of a frosty, uprooted fence post.

And spring will take wing when it's ready.

THE MAGIC AND MYSTERY OF EASTER

What does Easter mean to you? Did you gain your understanding of it from your childhood? Or from growth and enlightenment along the way?

When I look back to childhood memories of Easter, I see a simple little tarpapered house on the South Dakota prairie. Yet no special day was overlooked by our teacher mother, or diminished by this isolated location. When my two sisters and I awoke on Easter morning, we found beautiful eggs everywhere, real ones that our mother had boiled, colored and hidden, mostly inside the house. No matter how many each found, we divided them equally.

Later that morning when spring sun had warmed the air, we climbed to the top of the strawstack out by the barn, flung our small bodies onto the golden straw and spent several wonderful hours tossing rainbow-colored eggs high in the air, hoping they'd land on the straw so they wouldn't break. With a limited number of eggs, this activity created an exciting element of danger. If they broke, we'd have to eat them and the fun would end. If they landed in the stack, they might drift through the lightweight straw and disappear forever. Or until they became quite unappetizing.

Later, while our father re-stacked the straw we'd left vulnerable to the winds, we hid our eggs in mysterious places about the yard for each other to find - that old hide-and-seek game, now with tangible rewards.

All this activity did not leave our childhood Easters without spiritual significance. Anytime Sunday School was a reality on those wide prairie lands, our mother took us to church services, held from time to time in our little one-room country school named Harmony. I can still see a small, smiling man named Sylvan Hathaway waving his arms as if he were directing a huge choir, while his booming voice challenged the walls of Harmony with "Bringing in The Sheaves."

Somewhere in the reaches of my mind, I recall returning from Sunday School in ruffled pastel dresses our mother had sewn, and making desks of orange crates where we sat in the front yard in the warm sun and colored pictures of Bible characters.

From all this I sensed the importance, the magic of Easter. I learned about renewal of the earth when my sisters and I found the season's first johnny-jump-ups in a greening draw in Mr. Baker's pasture across the road. Life told its own story of rebirth when our mother, who colored only a few of the eggs the hens had laid, placed most of them under "setting hens," or in a kerosene-heated incubator. We found these eggs much more exciting than the hidden ones. These held hidden life.

Each day, we watched in quiet anticipation as if we might waken the chicks prematurely. While hens stirred the eggs in their nests, our mother daily turned those in the incubator, cleaned the wick and filled the small kerosene lamp that kept them warm and growing. Finally came the day. We gathered close to stare in hushed amazement as dozens of ordinary eggs popped open to free the fluffy yellow chicks. The air sang their peeping assurance that the springtime promise of ongoing life was here all along - in the simplest of everyday things.

Today, I still love the rainbow color of Easter eggs and the softness of baby chicks, the smell of rain and the first flower that blooms. And I've learned to make good hot cross buns.

I've also watched my spiritual self grow. I've discovered something I call a "divine nudge," a sense that I may be in a certain place at a certain time for reasons I may not immediately recognize. I've learned to be more aware of those nudges and that if I don't respond I may miss a chance to be more than I am, maybe to help someone.

But Easter issues its own call and people don't always hear it the same. Some see it as an inspiring time to nurture their spiritual selves; others envision little more than an elusive chocolate egg.

Singer Naomi Judd once explained why she responds as she does. "I'm a spiritual being having a human experience." I think I'll sign onto that concept. Sounds like one with a future.

MEN AND WOMEN

I suppose you think the differences between men and women are obvious? The basic similarity, a television news series suggests, is that "we're all made of bone, muscle and blood. Gender differences are governed by hormones."

Did some of our great scientists just wake up from a long winter's nap?

Still, I have a lot to learn about those little endocrines that affect our cellular activity, lead us around by the nose and sometimes impair good judgment. I enjoy the differences, though my effort to understand some of the points sometimes flounders. You'll probably note that shortly, depending on your gender.

Point #1: Men dislike asking directions when driving. No one explained what that had to do with hormones. Do male hormones carry compass capabilities? Or do they just trick men into thinking they can find the way themselves even if they've driven 50 miles down the road to Toolietown?

Point #2: Women are more articulate when their female hormone levels are at their peak. I didn't know that! You guys had better be careful when you argue with us. I suppose you wish I'd tell you something new?

Point #3: Men are better at spatial perception. I've always wondered how drivers' tests expect me to guess when I'm three car lengths behind the one roaring down the road ahead of me. How could I measure that unless I catch up first?

The only ticket I ever got was space related - improper parking. That was because the characters in front and back of me were incorrectly parked and I pulled into the only spot left between them. While I was in the restaurant, they sneaked off and left my car conspicuously alone in the center of two spaces. I plan to rely on my own spatial comprehension in the future.

Point #4: Men are more mechanical minded. Most women believe that depends on the equipment. The male understanding of the workings of cars, pickup trucks and snowmobiles is much more acute than it is of a dishwasher or a washing machine. Even getting a roll of toilet tissue onto its holder is sometimes too much of a challenge.

Still, I know a number of men, of my generation anyway, who handle vacuum cleaners very well, bless them. So I wouldn't limit their potential by trying to second guess them.

Point #5: As we grow older our hormones become more balanced, i.e., females grow more bold and confident about confronting the world, males more ready to back off from it.

Now there's a revelation! I've always wondered why I'd decide to write a book when I should be thinking of retiring. Or consent to lead a state writers organization. I just wish they'd explain how my body is to keep up with all the jobs my head says "yes" to. Are my hormones all stuck in my head?

Point #6: Women have a higher rate of mental-emotional problems than men. I think I'll leave my response to that one at the end of the 10-foot pole with which I wouldn't touch the subject.

The conclusion of these television sages was that men's and women's differences are complementary to each other; that together we fulfill the plan for mankind. I thought that understanding was accepted long ago. Or must we relearn it with every generation? And what's wrong with a little mystery, anyway?

A German man named Guillermo Mordillo said, "After God created the world, he made man and woman. Then, to keep the whole thing from collapsing, he invented humor."

Shall we laugh?

FINDING THE SELF

On Valentine's Day, love messages fly all directions in the form of cards, candy, flowers, jewelry and stuffed animals. Plus more than a few artful words. In the midst of all this a sobering phrase creeps into mind. "You can't find your self-worth in a love relationship. You must find yourself first."

I don't recall who said it, but it reminds me that not all share in the joy.

On what we perceive as a special day, some will feel loved, others rejected. Some will give love. Others, through a negative sense of self, will rebuff or blame someone else for problems and failures, then wonder why they feel rejected. Can it be the old saying is right in suggesting, "We get what we give?"

But if we're stuck inside ourselves, how do we break free?

I once heard a man speak on what he called, "the flip side of love," more commonly known as "rejection." We all know the feeling. It may be the most difficult thing we have to deal with in life.

"The irony is, we do it to ourselves," the man said.

Reject ourselves? How can that be? How strange that we'd create the very problem we struggle with. Doesn't it seem self-love would just come naturally, sort of a survival instinct? In that context, maybe. But relating to others is a different matter. Still, the fact remains, we can't feel very good toward someone else until we feel good about ourselves.

Where is that elusive sense of self, and how do we find it after our blunders, failures or wrongs to others?

Acknowledgment and regret are all we can offer. That speaker suggested that we then forgive ourselves. Only then can we escape self-inflicted chains and the wounds they cause. Only then can we open ourselves to the life and love we suspect may be enjoyed by others.

I believe the next move comes with accepting a challenge, then proving to ourselves, not someone else, that we can do what we decide to do. Maybe our hope is to acquire education, a particular job, paint a pleasing picture, write a book, win an award.

Or we may find fulfillment in being a caring parent, partner or friend. Another way to find self-worth is by helping others. The potential is endless. When we open ourselves to the world outside us, the world moves closer, grows more friendly and welcoming.

Personally, I've learned that when I feel depressed or negative, the only thing that can change it is to get busy at something that gives me a sense of accomplishment. It may be a small thing like cleaning a closet or writing in my journal, but it's a catalyst that gets me going. I start to feel good about myself. Energy begets energy and I'm on to bigger things. My failures or perceived failures of others fade into the background and lose their power.

I suspect I owe a good deal of this response pattern to my parents. I don't know how or where they acquired their attitude toward others, but as a child I never heard them criticize other people. I grew up believing something like, "You're OK. I'm OK," long before a book was written on the subject. Isn't it strange how a positive attitude toward others can reflect inward and give us an OK feeling about ourselves?

"The answer to rejection of self and others begins with forgiveness of self." I thought on the man's words. At home I pulled from my files a poem handed me many years ago. Called "The Key," these beautiful lines written by my sister express it simply and clearly.

All is forgiven. If man only knew;
the only thing left is
for you to forgive me,
and me forgive you.
But mostly the key,
if I could but see -
is for me to forgive
me.

THE CONFUSION OF SLEEP

Sleep, to me, is confusing.

While most writings on the subject consist of "how to" for those who can't, my problem is trying to figure out what's happening and how a state of repose can get one so disoriented. Psychiatrists from Freud forward have suggested it's healthy to pin one's idiosyncrasies on someone back in childhood if you can get away with it, so I'll assume that's where my affliction began.

I come from a family of nine children. I never realized there was a shortage of beds at our house, just a dearth of space in them.

"You sleep in the middle; you're smallest." This logic came from my two sisters, one on each side of me in age and in the bed we shared from early childhood until we left home. I wasn't sure I understood the rationale, but now suspect I was the only one gullible enough to buy such flimflam.

As my sisters grew and I tried to, I spent many cramped hours trying to mentally devise a subtle shuttle to ease one of them to the floor after she'd zonked out. I used to dream of being able to bend my knees the way God designed them. In puberty, my sisters' shapes were guided by hormones, but I'm convinced my body acquired its present arrangement from whatever space my parts could fit into between the figures on either side of me.

After I married, I was warm on one side only, and kept rotating like a chicken on a spit trying to keep the heat evenly distributed. Eventually, Ned's work began to involve considerable travel, so he bought me an electric blanket. By the time he returned from his first trip I had to confess psychological transference had taken place: I was in love with his warm, fuzzy surrogate.

Then there's the telephone.

"Don't get excited," I'm advised. "They'll call again."

Yet a ring in my sleep is like a command from heaven. I was in the kitchen with the minute timer caught on my ear one evening before I realized I'd fallen asleep on the sofa and the only message was that it was time to remove a casserole from the oven.

Animals too, are distorted in the twilight zone. When our son in his late teens slipped home quietly about midnight with a tiny orphan kitten under his arm, he decided it would be all right to turn it loose in the house until morning.

In the early dawn, I felt a weight hit my chest, heard what sounded like a vicious yowl and peeked through quivering lashes to perceive a magnified feline crouched for attack. One huge paw restrained its prey, while spear-sharp incisors aimed at my nose.

I jerked erect, arms flailing, and screamed hysterically, "Save me! Save me!"

While Ned summoned son and self-control to help tame the wild female in his bed, the poor little kitten bolted to the far end of the house, probably hoping he'd run into something more friendly. Like a German shepherd.

Although I don't come from a sleepwalking family, many encounters with confusion have occurred while on my feet and asleep. So in the years of Ned's traveling, he installed deadbolt locks on all our doors to keep me from charging forth to invite in Jack The Ripper. He also added peep-holes, an utter waste of course, since I couldn't focus my eyes enough to see after hitting the door at full speed.

In retrospect, it seems maybe I did need someone on each side of me at night in childhood. I might never have made it from there to my present keeper without my sideboard siblings. Besides, they warmed my feet in winter and kept me from falling out of bed for 18 years.

Lately, though, I'm growing a little concerned about my present guardian. One recent morning Ned commented at breakfast, "You know, I thought I got up twice last night. Then I realized I didn't get up the first time; I only got up the second time."

I wonder if sleep confusion might be contagious.

A LITTLE TOY TRUCK

In a pre-Christmas sermon one year, our pastor reminded, "A gift is only as good as the receiver." As usual, his ideas stimulate my thinking. This definitely is not a church where one goes to sleep.

Of course, there are all sorts of gifts. If the receiver doesn't like, can't eat, wear, or otherwise use the gift, the money spent for it may be wasted. But then there are gifts so thoughtful that they affect more than one life, and for a lifetime.

Years ago, I was told of a young boy in Nebraska who'd never received a Christmas gift. He didn't expect to. These were the days of the Great Depression. There was no Christmas tree, no decorations or gifts. Thankful for food, the boy's mother made a holiday dinner, sacrificing one of her hens who hadn't contributed to the egg supply with which she bought a few staple groceries now and then.

The hen was cooked in an old enameled pan with small bits of cloth pulled through the rusted holes to keep them from leaking. The mother had heard some folks repaired their pots with Mendits, tiny bolts that could extend the life of an aged kettle for years. But she had no money for such luxuries. She simply "made do."

The boy's oldest brother, 10 years his senior, married that year. The young wife, only 16 years old herself, was shocked to learn that her small brother-in-law had never known what it was to receive a Christmas gift. The thought tugged at her heart.

Somehow, either saving from her grocery money or from the loving grandfather who'd raised her, the girl found enough change to buy the boy a wonderful surprise that Christmas - a little blue toy truck.

Can you imagine what it would be like to be 11 years old before you knew how it felt to receive even one gift?

I was married many years before I heard my husband's touching childhood story. Today, Christmas to him is a beautiful time of love and generous giving. He starts early and often shops until Christmas Eve. His home, decorated inside and out, reflects a special joy.

And his sister-in-law? Sadly, she died of cancer a few years ago. Divorced from her husband by then, we changed her relationship to us from "sister-in-law" to "sister-in-love" in a poem I wrote for her. I'm told she treasured the poem. It was read at her funeral.

When I think of gifts at Christmas, I remember the one given us long ago by the birth of the Christ Child; then I think of His love in expression through a little blue truck given by a young girl to a boy who'd never received a Christmas gift. And who today gives me more than I deserve.

"A gift is only as good as the receiver."

I think also with gratitude of Rev. Earl whose fertile mind shares thoughtful and inspiring lessons with us all year long. So far, he hasn't put a stop to my giving some of them my own spin for a column now and then. At least he knows I'm listening. Thank you, Rev. Earl, for the gift of your wisdom, the spiritual nourishment, and your indomitable joy that survives the sorrows you also share.

I believe God gives all his children gifts of some sort, recognized or not. When I said that to one woman, she replied, "Oh, I didn't receive any gifts like that."

"What do you mean?" I asked.

"You know. I can't paint or sing or write."

"What are you good at? What do you like to do?" I asked.

"I'm only good at talking and laughing," she said, trying to make it a joke.

"Then maybe you could go visit someone who needs to talk and laugh?"

She looked surprised. I hope she put her gift to use. And I hope we'll all be good receivers this Christmas. Even a little toy truck can affect a lifetime. Or several.

IT'LL TURN UP

My mate believes things are never lost. They just aren't found.

When I wail, "I can't find it!" he responds with calm confidence, "It'll turn up."

It doesn't matter if it's my car keys, my wedding ring, a towel bar I thought I remembered buying, or the special coffee measure I had marked for the 30-cup pot. And he's right. Eventually, they all turn up. If he's so sure though, I wish he'd tell me when. And while he's at it, where?

The irony of all this is that on a recent anniversary he gave me a card noting my ability to find things. Like his socks, matching clothes items, and the nerve to ask directions.

I can also find a way to lose things.

My mother once recalled that when I was a child I hid objects so they wouldn't get lost. You guessed it. I forgot where I hid them. Were they lost? Of course not. They just weren't found yet.

Last week I went to a local pharmacy to get a prescription filled. But where was it? I searched every pocket and zipper in my purse, pants, and shirt. My friendly pharmacist watched with compassion while he waited.

"Maybe I changed purses," I mumbled. He smiled the indulgent smile of all males who understand deep in their beings the disaster potential in a woman changing purses.

"I"ll find it," I assured him. At home, after a thorough search the prescription turned up. Guess where? In the medicine cabinet. What's so strange about that? Isn't the medicine cabinet the safest place for a prescription? Where else would you put it?

A few weeks ago I lost my car keys. My house and mailbox keys were on the same ring.

If my mate hadn't had another set in his pants pocket, we'd have been sleeping under the stars and eating raw veggies with the grasshoppers in our garden.

After asking Ned for his keys every day or so for a couple of weeks, I announced, "I want my own set. I feel helpless and dependent this way."

"Okay," he said, possibly more than a little worried I might lose his keys too.

We went to get new ones made. Of course the ignition key has a computer chip in it.

"Sorry, but it'll be $15.00 for this one," said the sympathetic man at the garage. After I paid him, he smiled knowingly. "You'll probably find the other one now."

Next morning, I was looking through a purse I'd searched a dozen times from one end to the other. Suddenly, my fingers touched something hard and irregular in shape in a small zippered pocket. I suppose you think the keys were there all along?

As it turned out, I fell into an entire week of lucky finds. While looking through a drawer in the laundry room that holds myriads of mysteries, I came upon not one, but two towel bars that just match the ones in the front bathroom! Our guests are gone now, so there's no need for the extra bars. Maybe we'll install them before their next visit. If I can get Ned to help me before I hide or misplace them again.

And that's not all. The coffee measure for the 30-cup pot fell out of a paper cup I removed from a cabinet last week. I'd really wanted it for the family reunion a month ago. Oh, we had coffee. Ned made it without the measure. The lost wedding ring, I found under the kitchen island cabinet. Why was it there? Who knows? Rings roll.

Finally, just so you won't think I'm totally brain-dead, I want you to know things that turn up aren't always lost ones. Once, when readying our furniture for a move to a new home, I found a $20 bill in the bottom of a dresser drawer. I'm not complaining, but I have no idea who put it there. And the other day, I pulled on a pair of jeans and found a $10 bill in the watch pocket. How did it get there? Who knows? Matter of fact, who cares? The important thing is, it turned up.

WHAT'S FOREVER FOR?

A few years ago there was a song that went something like, "Doesn't anybody ever mean 'forever' anymore? If they don't, tell me, what's 'forever' for?"

I liked the song a lot. It made the charts but was not quite so popular as I'd hoped it might be. Today, with the light-hearted encounters that lead to parents without love creating children without parents, I wonder if "forever" has now been compressed into minutes.

The thought both challenges and frustrates. "I'll love you forever" didn't used to mean "I'll love you until I don't find you lovable." It meant "I'll love you even if you aren't always lovable." Or "until you're lovable again." It was valid because few of us are always lovable.

A magazine article once explained that love can be divided into two types of chemical behavior. The first, infatuation, is triggered by a brainbath of adrenaline-like neurochemicals which may last three to six years. Then many go off searching for it again, becoming "love junkies."

There's another type of chemical reward, however, for those who stick around for the experience, according to Helen Fisher, Ph.D., author of *Anatomy of Love*. It's created by a new brainbath of endorphins that don't give up on us so soon.

Mark Goulston, M.D., professor of psychiatry at the University of California, explains it this way, "Adrenaline-based love is all about ourselves - we like being in love. With endorphins, we like loving."

I know a few people who've endorsed the endorphins. My parents, for instance, had been married 62 years when my father died. They never had a lot of material things, and there were rocky spots along the way. But I always remember the things they laughed about together. And they laughed a lot. Sometimes I suspect love and laughter walk hand-in-hand. Both seem to have a healing touch.

I believe they healed my mother's tragic injuries after the auto accident when doctors said she couldn't live and ambulance attendants thought at first she shouldn't have.

The wonder of it, to me, is that my father, whose response to life sometimes hurt him as much as it did others, was aware of the great power of love and laughter probably more than anyone I've known.

Maybe that's what my mother knew.

In memory, I still see the two 80-year-olds sharing a goodnight kiss as she lay in that hospital bed. I remember how the kiss lingered. I recall the warm light in my mother's eyes and the shared chuckle as the kiss ended.

Maybe that's what made it possible for my mother a year or so later to say with a happy smile, "If I keep improving at this rate, I'll be in perfect health by the time I die!" And for my father to play "You Are My Sunshine" on his harmonica that morning, then fill the room with gleeful energy as he broke into a whirling, jigging dance.

Maybe this elderly couple knew what forever's for.

NOTES AND ACKNOWLEDGMENTS

Some resource materials for this book were obtained from the following publications:

U.S. Department of The Interior, Bureau of Land Management

U.S. Department of The Interior, National Park Service

Wyoming Highway Department

The Ranger–Riverton, Wyoming daily newspaper

Devils Tower: Stories in Stone, by Mary Alice Gunderson–High Plains Press

South Pass and Its Tales, by James L. Sherlock–Wolverine Gallery

Knights of The Broadax, by Joan Trego Pinkerton–The Caxton Printers, Ltd.

I Didn't Know That About Wyoming, by Lavinia Dobler–Wolverine Gallery

Other information was obtained from Loren Jost, Curator, The Riverton Museum

The Wyoming Dinosaur Center, Thermopolis, Wyoming

* * * * *

The story, Tractor Tales, was previously published in *Leaning into The Wind*, Houghton-Mifflin

The poem, Elk Mountain Jimmy, was previously published in The Casper Star-Tribune

The poem, Independence Rock–1843, was previously published in *If You Would Love Wyoming*, WYOPoets chapbook